GRAPHIC
INTRODUCTION
TO PROGRAMMING

PRINCIPLES OF COMPUTER-AIDED DESIGN

A Series by

Yehuda E. Kalay
School of Architecture and Environmental Design
State University of New York, Buffalo

Graphic Introduction To Programming
Computability of Design

GRAPHIC INTRODUCTION TO PROGRAMMING

Yehuda E. Kalay
School of Architecture and Environmental Design
State University of New York
Buffalo, New York

A Volume in a Series entitled Principles of Computer-Aided Design

A WILEY-INTERSCIENCE PUBLICATION
JOHN WILEY & SONS
New York / Chichester / Brisbane / Toronto / Singapore

Copyright © 1987 by Yehuda E. Kalay
Published by John Wiley & Sons, Inc.

Library of Congress Cataloging in Publication Data:

Kalay, Yehuda E.
  Graphic introduction to programming.
  Bibliography: p.
  Includes index.
  1. Electronic digital computers—Programming.
2. Computer graphics.   I. Title.
QA76.6.K3416   1987   620′.00425′0285   86-26746
ISBN 0-471-85389-5

Printed in the United States of America

10 9 8 7 6 5 4 3 2 1

To the memory of my father
Izchack E. Kalay 1906 to 1987

SERIES PREFACE

Computers have made their debut as design tools in many engineering disciplines, providing designers with flexible means to represent design products. In that capacity they have already demonstrated their utility in improving the productivity and the quality of the production end of the design process, much like word processors have improved the production of documents in offices.

A growing number of researchers, developers, and users of computer-aided design (CAD) systems, however, have reached the conclusion that the utility of computers in design is far from what it might become, if their use were extended over the design process as a whole, including the complete, accurate, and efficient representation of the designed artifacts and the processes that are employed in their conception and creation.

This series of five books is intended to help realize the potential of CAD, through the introduction—in an integrative form—of principles, methodologies, and practices that underlie CAD. It is intended to be used by people who wish to engage in the process of research, development, and maintenance of the new generation of CAD systems. Since the current cadre of people involved with R&D in CAD is relatively small, the series assumes that the reader has no particular knowledge of the field and thus it can be used as a text for beginners. The topics it introduces progress, nevertheless, rapidly toward the frontiers of CAD and thus make the series useful as a text for advanced courses and as reference for professionals.

The first volume, *Graphic Introduction to Programming,* introduces the basic concepts of computing that are needed to master the tool—namely, the computer. These concepts include programming, structured problem solving, and interactive computer graphics. Programming is the means through which computers are instructed how to perform the desired tasks. Structured problem solving, through algorithm design and analysis, encourages a disciplined approach to the design process as a whole and to computer-aided design software development in particular. Given the established manner of communicating design between humans, and because of the ease with which graphic and pictorial information can be disseminated compared to text and numerals, computer graphics have become the standard means of interaction with CAD systems. These three topics have been integrated and are covered through learning the programming language Pascal. This language has certain features that qualify it for this task, which include ease of comprehension, enforcing good programming practices, availability on most computers, and provision of dynamic memory management facilities.

The second volume, *Modeling Objects and Environments,* introduces the concepts of modeling real-world phenomena in the computer's memory. It covers a set of methods and techniques for representing the physical environment as symbol structures that are understood and can be manipulated by computers. The book includes the study of data structures that are particularly suitable for representing two- and three-dimensional artifacts, and operating on these structures in a way that preserves their semantic integrity. The book covers the formative and other attributes of objects, such as topology, geometry, transformations, assemblies, and general database query/update operations.

The third volume, *Modeling Design Processes,* is concerned with the representation of design as a problem-solving process. The two essential components of CAD covered include the generation and the evaluation of alternative design solutions, represented through the modeling concepts introduced in the second volume. The study of solution generation covers all design phases, including preconcept, conceptual, and detailed design. It is introduced through techniques such as knowledge representation and search strategies and relies on selected practices from artificial intelligence, database theory, linear and dynamic programming, operations research, and optimization theory. All of these topics are covered in sufficient detail for the comprehension of the central topics in the book, though of course they do not attempt to be a substitute for formal texts in their respective disciplines. The theoretical treatment of the topics covered by the book is complemented by examples written in PROLOG, a programming language that has some powerful features useful for logic representation and manipulation. For the benefit of readers who are not familiar with PROLOG, an appendix introduces the basics of this language.

The fourth volume, *Performance Measurement Applications,* presents an assortment of task-specific applications that draw upon the model of the designed artifact and provide the designer and the knowledge-based CAD system with a variety of evaluative, simulative, and tabulative measures of the artifacts' expected performances. Written by noted experts in their respective disciplines, the applications present both state-of-the-art knowledge in specific fields relating to CAD and an integrative approach to employing computers as design consultants.

The fifth volume, *Computability of Design,* completes the series by reviewing the key topics that were presented, and by raising the fundamental issues of design computation: How can design processes be mathematically modeled? What is design knowledge, and how can it be computed? How can the design process as a whole be computed? Alternatively, how can particular design tasks be computationally assisted? This volume is based on a symposium that was held in Buffalo, New York, in December 1986, where noted experts discussed the feasibility, utility, and desirability of various approaches to the computation of design.

The series as a whole is concerned with the principles of CAD, rather than with an exhaustive survey of techniques, practices, and existing systems. Its goal is to educate students, researchers, and professionals, who will develop the CAD systems of the future and who will maintain them. It is intended to be used by designers in many engineering disciplines, rather than by computer scientists alone. It may, however, be of considerable interest to computer scientists too, by exposing them to the computational concerns of design professionals.

It is recommended that the books be used in sequence, but this is not a prerequisite for their utility. Neither is adherence to the programming languages Pascal and PROLOG, which are used to exemplify the theory. It is the concepts and principles presented in the series that are of primary importance, and they transcend the technologies and techniques used for their implementation.

YEHUDA E. KALAY

Buffalo, New York
February 1987

PREFACE

Computers are rapidly changing the methods and practices used by most engineering disciplines for the design and manufacture of physical artifacts. Consequently, there is a growing need for trained people who can contribute to the development of computer-aided design (CAD) software, as well as a need for people who can use that software effectively. This volume introduces the reader to the principles upon which computer-aided design software is founded.

In general, design can be considered a process of search for an optimal or satisfactory solution to a stated problem. The process requires a means for generating solutions and a way of evaluating solutions according to some criteria. Unlike manual design processes, computer-aided design involves the *representation* of design solutions in the computer's memory. In addition, it involves the issue of the human–machine *interface*.

The purpose of this first volume in the series is to serve as an introduction to the principles of computer-aided design and as a textbook for an introductory course in programming and interactive computer graphics. It attempts to unify in a single volume the fundamentals of structured programming, the syntax of programming in Pascal, and the principles of interactive computer graphics that are applied in displaying and manipulating two-dimensional images. The programming language Pascal has been chosen because it is well suited for computer-aided design and computer graphics, it is easy to learn, and it has a rigorous structure that induces good programming practices and facilitates structured problem solving. Since the major concern of this book is CAD, rather than programming, it addresses only those features of Pascal that have been deemed relevant. It is recommended, therefore, that this text be accompanied by the *Pascal Manual and Report* by Jensen and Wirth (published by Springer-Verlag), which can serve as a reference and provide additional explanations where needed.

Computer graphics, however, are usually considered to require a much higher level of computer literacy than programming, and their study is, therefore, typically deferred until the student has mastered that skill. Hence the study of computer programming is usually divorced from any graphic applications. Programming examples and exercises are based, instead, on numerical and text manipulation problems.

For students and professionals in disciplines such as architecture and engineering, which emphasize graphic communication, deferring graphics in favor of numerical problem solving is undesirable and unnecessary. Most, if not all, of the concepts of computer programming can be illustrated much more effectively and intuitively with graphic examples. The concept of iteration, for instance, can be easily illustrated through the drawing of an approximate circle made of many small straight line segments, and recursion is the hallmark of the famous Sierpiski curve. Furthermore, the satisfaction a student derives from the ability to generate pictures on a CRT screen, practically from day one, may enhance the learning process and improve retention of knowledge. The complexity and the significance of these pictures gradually increase through the book, building up to a simple yet effective drafting system that embodies everything the student has learned through this process. The exercises unify the components of the learning process into one whole.

The introduction to graphics in this book is by no means a substitute for a full text on computer graphics. Its intent is merely to introduce the student to the concepts of image generation and manipulation. The interested reader is advised to consult the Bibliography for other references on this subject.

From the student's point of view, this book is a step-by-step introduction to the design and development of computer tools for interactive drafting. Starting with simple line drawing, the student will gain the skills needed to write software that is capable of highly interactive entry, manipulation, storage, and display of two-dimensional images on a graphic display terminal. The book should be read sequentially, as each chapter builds on the knowledge acquired in the preceding ones.

The book consists of four parts, preceded by an Introduction and followed by the Appendices. Each part addresses a single subject through several chapters. The Introduction considers notions such as problem solving and programming and surveys briefly the history of computer-aided design. The first part deals with the basic concepts of programming, including sequential instruction processing and the important roles played by names and values. The second part introduces control structures, including repetition constructs, decision constructs, and partitioning constructs (procedures and functions). The third part develops the skills for data structuring, through such topics as constants, enumerated (user-defined) types, arrays, records, and lists. The fourth part deals with the manipulation of text—within the program, its communication to the terminal, and to files—and contains a conclusion. Appendices on Pascal keywords and graphic display drivers appear at the end of the book.

Each chapter in the book is organized in three parts:

1. A theoretical problem and its logical solution.

2. Pascal syntax to encode the solution.
3. Graphic application and examples.

To facilitate portability of the graphics package, the display drivers are presented as a set of external procedures, to be loaded together with each program. The drivers may be implemented in various ways; one implementation that will run on most TEKTRONIX-emulating hardware is described in Appendix B.

The programming examples in this book were written in Berkley Pascal Version 1.1, under the Berkley UNIX 4.3 operating system.

Books of this nature are not developed in a vacuum. They require a nurturing and supportive environment, where ideas are generated, discussed, and tested. The environment that supported the development of the methodologies and techniques that are presented in this book has been the Computer-Aided Design and Graphics Laboratory of the School of Architecture and Environmental Design at the State University of New York at Buffalo. I am indebted to my colleagues and students who criticized, tested, and otherwise helped in shaping the methodologies presented here. I am also grateful to the departmental, school, and the university administrations for providing the much needed support and encouragement for undertaking this task.

The production of the book itself owes much to C. Harvey Lichtblau, who edited this volume and improved its readability and consistency; and to L. Donald Steiger for his continuous effort and thoroughness in the production of this difficult manuscript. Many thanks to both.

YEHUDA E. KALAY

Buffalo, New York
February 1987

CONTENTS

PART TWO CONTROL

PART THREE DATA STRUCTURES

INTRODUCTION

People have always striven to modify and adapt the environment they inhabit so it will provide better shelter, food, and recreation. At first people made progress only by accidental discoveries, then by purposeful trial and error. Although progress by trial and error was slow and costly, it led to the development of some sophisticated tools and environments, ranging from clocks to farm machinery and from Gothic cathedrals to planned cities.

The growing complexity of tools and environments required, nevertheless, a different approach to their development. This approach was to enable tool developers to comprehend (a) the multitude of components of an artifact or building working in concert and (b) their expected impact on the environment. The sixteenth century is noted for the invention of engineering and architectural drawings, along with their use as a means to represent and communicate hypothetical adaptations of tools and environments. This separation of the search for a solution from its physical realization allowed not only the development of much more complex artifacts than ever possible before, but also the selective implementation of only those solutions that seemed most suitable, at a considerable reduction in development cost and time. It has also created a new discipline, called *design*. Its practitioners were required to be capable of technical innovation and of predicting the future performance of their creations. Since both innovation and prediction are based on creativity and judgment (two of the most distinguished human traits), designers have attained the status reserved for artists. Yet, this has also been the source of many products and environments that failed to meet their designers' expectation.

The inherent uncertainties associated with creativity and judgment make the development of new artifacts and environments difficult and undermine the education of new design professionals. The attempt to understand how designers work and how to teach design principles to students is the subject of inquiry of a relatively new discipline known as *design theory*. It has also guided the search for tools that will help designers accomplish their tasks more effectively and predictably.

The advent of digital computers now provides design theorists and tool builders with the opportunity to make significant progress on both fronts. On the one hand, it provides us with a machine that can mimic, under certain conditions, human thought processes and thus serve as an extrospective examiner of these processes. On the other hand, it can assume some of the responsibilities of human designers and speed up some others. Yet, even though design theory has made much progress since computers have been introduced as its main tool of inquiry, we are still far from really understanding how designers work.

Nevertheless, some advances have been made. We now have at least a general understanding of the design process, portrayed as a hierarchical, goal-directed problem-solving activity. Furthermore, we are able to simulate environments that do not yet exist physically (which is what the design process is all about) and test their expected behavior. The computer allows us to view potential environments and explore their properties, just as the telescope allows astronomers to explore distant galaxies that are not visible to the unaided eye.

Computer-Aided Design (CAD) is, then, a utilization of the computer's abilities to simulate both the design process itself and the artifacts being designed. The computer can be made to assume different roles in the design process and thereby either relieve the human designer from certain responsibilities or aid the designer in making decisions along the way.

In order to identify the various roles computers can play in the design of physical artifacts, it is useful first to look at design as a problem-solving process whose goal is to find a way to change the current "state of the world" into one that is better suited for some purpose.

☐ THE PROBLEM-SOLVING MODEL OF DESIGN

Let us construct a model of design as a problem-solving process. The basis for this model is the assumption that for any problem we may define a solution space, which is the domain that includes all the possible solutions to the problem. Consider for example, the game of chess: At any point in the game there is a finite number of permissible moves. The chess player must attempt to evaluate these moves and choose the one most likely to lead to winning the game. In general, problem solving can be viewed as a process of searching through alternative solutions within the solution space in order to find one that meets certain criteria. The word *search* is used here in a metaphoric sense to describe a process of seeking and evaluating alternative solutions.

In this vein, a consumer looking to buy a car can also be said to be searching a "solution space" that consists of all the car makes that fulfill his needs and that he can afford. In contrast to this explicit solution space, the solution space searched by a design process is *implicit* since design problems usually involve seeking a solution that does not exist yet. This raises the question of how potential solutions may be produced for evaluation. The evaluation part must, therefore, be complemented by a solution-generating part—that is, a procedure that synthesizes potential solutions to the problem. If the solution-generating part is successful, the potential solutions will include at least one that complies with all the constraints of the design problem, achieves all its goals, and is technically and economically feasible.

Computers can be employed in various roles in this design model. They can be made to perform both the generation of potential solutions and their evaluation, a method which, when iterated, may eventually produce a solution to the given problem. In this case the human designer is completely excluded from the design process, and his role is limited to formulating the problem and presenting it to the computer for solution.

Alternatively, if we do not wish to or know how to make the computer generate potential solutions, we can include the human designer in the synthesis/analysis cycle as the generator of potential solutions and use the computer only for certain evaluations. The problem that arises in this case is, how will the designer communicate his generated potential solutions to the computer for analysis?

If we do not wish to bother with such communication problems, or if we cannot instruct the computer how to evaluate the potential solutions (e.g., their aesthetic qualities), then we can limit the role of the computer to a representational medium that replaces traditional paper-and-pencil drawing. The ability of the computer to represent the designed artifact in its three-dimensional form is far superior to the conventional method of representation by two-dimensional projections, such as the floorplans and elevations of a building. Three-dimensional representation allows the computer to test for interference between the pipes and ducts of the building or detect collisions between moving parts of a machine. It enables the computer to generate perspective, axonometric, and other views of the designed artifact automatically; and it allows the designer to "walk through" the building and get an impression of it, or to simulate the operation of a machine such as the tool path of a numerically controlled milling machine.

Finally, the computer can be used to generate shop drawings automatically, along with the many schedules and parts lists that accompany them. The computer can also be used to manage the design and production process as a whole, such as by identifying the critical path in a sequence of activities.

□ BRIEF HISTORY OF COMPUTER-AIDED DESIGN

Computers were first introduced in the design process in the late 1950s as aids in performing the many calculations involved in analysis of engineered products. Computers calculated the structural behavior of artifacts, fluid flow, and thermal conductivity.

The early computer-aided design systems were aimed at improving the accuracy of various predictive models, using the computer's ability to handle many numbers very quickly. Little or no attention was given to the issue of data entry; it was assumed that design was performed in its traditional manner, except that at specific points in its progress some numerical quantities, representing the data for a set of equations, were taken off drawings and fed manually to the computer for specific processing.

Over the years, the tasks that could be processed by computers have multiplied and have been refined. Having learned how to solve many specific tasks, the developers of computer-aided design systems turned their attention to the growing problems of data collection and entry.

Then a new development occurred in the field of computing—a development that was crucial in bringing computer-aided design to its present state. This development was the realization that computers are capable of representing images as well as text and numbers. A new field, called *computer graphics*, was conceived at MIT in the late 1950s. It was, however, the work, of Steven Coons and his colleagues at MIT in the early 1960s that put computer graphics on the track that led to its current important status.

Coons developed a scenario that has guided most of the research and development in computer-aided design so far. According to his plan, design was to be done entirely on an interactive graphic terminal, using the computer to represent and manipulate the designed artifact. Since the entire artifact was already represented in the computer's memory, it could be used to extract the data required for a particular analysis automatically. Such analysis could be initiated by the designer or by the computer itself, and the results could be presented to the designer almost instantaneously and in the most convenient form. Upon completion of the design, the computer would be instructed to produce drawings, parts lists, and other production documentation, including fabrication instructions for numerically controlled machine tools. The computer, according to this scenario, becomes the engineer's "workstation," at which he can develop a product from start to finish.

The only design field in which Coons' scenario has been fully implemented so far is Electrical Engineering. More specifically, the design and fabrication of integrated circuits is now entirely computer-aided. This development owes as much to the work of Mead and Conway (who formalized integrated circuits design check rules) as to the many developments in computer-aided design, computer graphics, and computer science in general. In this capacity, computers are now used to interpret high-level design schemas, automatically generate and place electronic components, connect them, and simulate their performance.

Other fields of design are still a long way from realizing Coons' scenario. In architecture and engineering computers are limited, by and large, to the representation and analysis of design solutions developed manually. Automatic generation of design solutions has, so far, been limited to very well-defined problems. Furthermore, computer-aided integration of decisions made by many designers collaborating on one project is nonexistent. Yet, thanks to the work done by many researchers, Coons' scenario may be closer to realization in these "hard" design fields as well. Some examples of these advances include Nicholas Negroponte's and his MIT "Architecture Machine" group's proposed partnership approach to design, in which only those components of the process most suitable for automation are computerized, while others are left for the designer to perform. Charles Eastman and his Carnegie-Mellon University (CMU) "GLIDE" group proposed some models for representing the semantics, as well as the syntax, of large engineering and architectural artifacts and how their complex interrelationships could be managed automatically. William Mitchell and his UCLA colleagues demonstrated how the rules that underlie certain well-known architectural styles can be written down and reused, through a formalism known as "shape grammars." Steven Fenves and his colleagues at CMU demonstrated how certain decision-making processes that are employed in civil engineering can be made explicit and embedded in "expert systems" that mimic the behavior of human engineers.

All these developments, and many more, will advance the state of the art of CAD and will lead to a new generation of engineering workstations that will contain specific knowledge about the tasks for which they are employed, as well as the designed artifacts themselves. Thus they may become an active partner in the design process, rather than mere drafting and analysis aids. They may be able to check the progress of the design, suggest alternative courses of action, and guarantee that some predefined rules of consistency are preserved. Such systems will aid the *designer*, rather than the draftsperson, at a much higher level in the design process hierarchy than the current systems do and allow him to concentrate more fully on the critical design issues themselves.

PART ONE

BASIC CONCEPTS

1

PROGRAMMING

Programming is the generic term for a collection of practices and techniques that allow us to transform the wires, transistors, and electrical currents that comprise a computer into a sophisticated tool capable of the purposeful behavior that we call problem solving. This transformation has many levels. At the highest level it may involve the formulation of a solution procedure as a sequential list of instructions. At the lowest level it involves the on/off switching of electrical signals. Typically this transformation, which reduces the high-level problem-solving activity of the programmer's mind into the electrical pulses of the digital computer, is resolved into a chain of smaller transformations, each reducing the former into simpler, more elementary instructions, down to the electrical current switching level.

Some of these transformations—such as formulating the solution to a given problem—are performed by the programmer. Others are performed by the various systems that comprise a computer. In order to better understand the nature of these transformations, let us consider first the components that comprise a digital computer.

☐ HARDWARE

A general-purpose computer typically consists of three main interconnected units:

1. The central processing unit (CPU).
2. The memory unit.
3. The input/output unit.

An action by the computer is initiated in response to instructions issued by a user. If the instructions are in the form of *alphanumerics*—that is, text composed of letters and numerals—then they are typed in on a keyboard. If the instructions are in the form of *graphics,* they are communicated to the computer by placing a pointing device called the *cursor* at the desired screen location and registering that location.

A variety of input/output devices are available, each suited for certain applications. There are alphanumeric terminals that use paper on which the user's instructions and the computer's response are typed; there are alphanumeric terminals that use a televisionlike screen called a *CRT* (cathode-ray tube), and many more. All of these serve as interface between the computer and human users—for entering data and reviewing output—so they are all known by the generic name of *terminals.*

Of particular interest to us are terminals capable of drawing lines and shaded images. These are called *graphic terminals;* generally they can be switched, upon instructions issued by the user or by the computer, between *alphanumeric mode* and *graphics mode.* In alphanumeric mode, the graphic terminal behaves just like an alphanumeric terminal; it interprets the electrical currents as characters. In graphic mode, it is a true graphic device. According to its instructions, it may interpret the electrical currents as screen locations, visible lines of transition from one screen location to another, or varying intensities of an individual point—called a *pixel* (picture element)—on the screen.

The *central processing unit,* or CPU, is the heart of the computer—or rather its brain. Its functions are to decode the instruction it receives from the terminals, store and retrieve data from the memory, and carry out the arithmetical computations. Physically, the CPU is a large collection of transistors embedded in a silicon chip of minute size.

The *main memory unit* stores the information delivered to it by the CPU. It is organized as a large array of individual cells, each designated by a unique address. The information stored within each cell may be an item of data, an encoded instruction, or the encoded address of another memory cell. The main memory is limited in size, and its contents are lost whenever the computer is switched off or loses power. To remedy these deficiencies, *auxiliary memory units* are usually added to the basic configuration. These units consist of magnetic disks or tapes; they are capable of storing vast amounts of information, and they retain the information when power is switched off.

Information can be retrieved from main memory much more quickly than from auxiliary memory. Therefore, the CPU typically manages information in such a way that all data required for a particular computation is stored in main memory. When the computation is done, the data in main memory may be replaced, as needed, with other data from the auxiliary memory.

The particular structure of a computer—known as its *architecture*—varies from one model of computer to another, and there are many more circuits than we can discuss here. This generalized discussion does give at least a functional outline of most present-day computer systems.

□ SOFTWARE

To illustrate the working of a computer and the chain of transformations that reduce purposeful problem solving into electrical pulses, let us consider the simple task of drawing a line on the screen of a graphic terminal.

The Programmer's Role

The first problem that you, as the programmer, must solve is: "How can I instruct the computer to draw a line?" Let's assume that the computer can handle the mechanics of drawing the line, provided that we tell it where to begin and where to end. Then the problem has been transformed into: "How can I specify the two endpoints of the line I wish drawn?" To aid us in specifying points, the screen of a graphic terminal is composed of a coordinate grid in which points are identified by means of two numerical values, usually in the range of 0 to 1023. The first value, the *X coordinate,* corresponds to the horizontal displacement of the point from the lower-left corner of the screen; the second value, the *Y coordinate,* corresponds to its vertical displacement. As depicted in Figure 1.1, a line can now be defined as a set of two points, given their *X* and *Y* coordinates.

You can now solve the line-drawing problem with these steps:

1. Move to point ⟨100,200⟩— that is, get to this point but do not trace the route on the screen.
2. Draw to point ⟨500,600⟩—that is, get to the new point and trace the route on the screen.

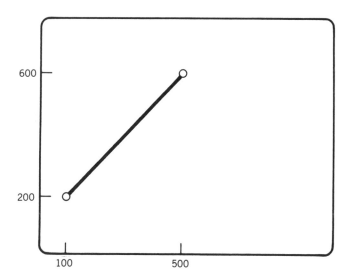

Figure 1.1. Defining a line as two pairs of coordinate values.

This two-step sequence of instructions is an *algorithm*—that is, a concise, stepwise, unambiguous, and effective solution to a problem.

Your task is not yet completed. The algorithm must be translated into a language that is understood by the machine. Unfortunately, English—or any other natural language for that matter—is not precise enough to convey instructions unambiguously to a computer. Consider the statement "Time flies like an arrow." Does it mean that a species of insects called "time flies" prefer arrows as their diet, or that our temporal existence passes quickly?

Programming languages overcome this problem, making it possible to convey instructions precisely and unambiguously. Many such languages have been developed, most of them with specific goals in mind. One of them, Pascal, is most suitable for computer-aided design. This programming language, invented by Niklaus Wirth in 1968, was named after Blaise Pascal—the eighteenth-century French scientist who invented, among other things, the mechanical adding machine.

Pascal is a high-level programming language of the Algol family. A *high-level* programming language is closer to a natural language such as English than to the instructions that actually make the computer operate. It allows programmers to write precise instructions that can be interpreted and translated automatically into machine instructions, yet it has features that will make the writing of such instructions easy. Also, a high-level language allows the program to be executed on many different computers, not just the one we happened to be using when we first wrote the program.

Let's assume that you have already mastered the two arts of devising algorithms to solve problems in CAD and translating those algorithms into Pascal. You have come up with an appropriate Pascal program containing the instructions to draw a line. The instructions have been translated into a programming language and have been given to the computer for execution. What happens next?

The Computer's Role

The instructions given to the computer do not go unheeded. They are immediately interpreted by a program that is always running and that makes the computer respond when instructed. This program is called the *operating system*. Its task is to oversee all the operations performed by the computer.

When the operating system recognizes that the instructions are a program written in Pascal, it invokes another program, called the *Pascal compiler*.

The compiler's task is to *parse* the program, transforming the high-level instructions into simple, low-level instructions that will be understood by this particular computer. The steps in this transformation are depicted in Figure 1.2.

Suppose the Pascal instructions were:

1. MOVETO ⟨100,200⟩;
2. DRAWTO ⟨500,600⟩;

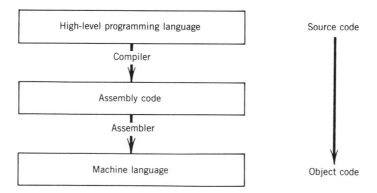

Figure 1.2. The program transformation chain.

The compiler may translate these statements into:

1. Turn the electron beam off.
2. Move the electron beam to screen location ⟨100,200⟩.
3. Turn the electron beam on.
4. Move the electron beam to screen location ⟨500,600⟩.
5. Stop.

If there are some errors in the program, the compiler may be unable to understand the instructions. In that case, it will make its best effort to indicate what went wrong, and in some cases it may even attempt to correct the errors. In most cases, however, it will be unable to continue and will stop, reporting the error.

If the compiler succeeds in parsing the program, it will generate a set of instructions that are functionally equivalent to the Pascal instructions but are written in a lower-level language called *assembly* language. The assembly code may contain instructions that are particular to the machine being used, so it is no longer portable to other computers.

The assembly code is not the end of the chain of transformations. This code still has to be translated into binary *machine code* that may look something like this:

```
01001100110  (turn off electron beam).
01100100110  (move electron beam to certain screen location).
01001100100  (turn on electron beam).
01110001110  (move electron beam to new screen location).
```

After this step has been successfully completed, the end of the chain is reached at last. The machine code will cause certain currents to be turned on or off, deflecting the electron beam in the graphic terminal to the correct screen locations, and the line will be drawn as desired.

Debugging

The above chain of operations is highly stylized and resembles only metaphorically the much more complex sequence of actions that really occurs in a modern digital computer. However, it does convey the essential steps in this rather long and complicated sequence of actions—generating the problem-solving algorithm, translating it into a program written in a high-level programming language, compiling and translating the program into low-level machine code, and executing the program.

In most cases, a single pass through this chain is insufficient. If the compiler reports any errors, then the programmer must correct them and start the cycle again. When the compilation succeeds and a line is actually traced on the screen, the programmer may find that the result is not what was intended. The instructions must then be revised, an act that requires starting the cycle all over.

This iteration through a cycle of transformations is known as *debugging;* the programmer rids the program of "bugs" until it executes without error. The program is then completed and is said to be "running."

The computer must process the program in two distinct stages within the cycle of transformations. First, the computer must translate the *source code*—that is, the set of instructions written in a high-level programming language—into *object code*— that is, the corresponding instructions in low-level language. Second, the computer must *execute* the object code, carrying out the encoded instructions to produce the actions specified by the programmer.

These two stages of processing give rise to two kinds of errors:

1. Syntactical errors, which prevent proper translation, as we have seen before.
2. Logical errors, due to some oversight on the part of the programmer in solving the problem. This is the more serious and more difficult kind of error to find and correct, and this is where most of the program development time is actually spent.

While it is important to understand the working of the computer, our main concerns in this book, and generally in CAD software development, are the problem-solving and high-level programming parts of the program transformation chain. The problem-solving part deals with constructing a logical, algorithmic solution to a given problem. The high-level programming part deals with the correct, efficient, and readable encoding of the algorithm into a programming language such as Pascal.

□ THE PASCAL PROGRAM

We have described the logical part of solving the simple problem of drawing a line on the screen of a graphic terminal. The solution involved using a coordinate system and specifying the line to be drawn as a set of two points. How is this solution encoded in Pascal? To see how it is done, we must first understand the general structure of a Pascal program.

Basically, any computer program is a list of instructions. When the computer executes the program, it starts at the first instruction and executes every instruction in turn until all have been executed. The computer is capable of handling a list containing thousands of instructions. However, to make the program meaningful from the programmer's point of view, this general pattern must be broken down in a hierarchical manner into what is known as a *structure*.

The evolution of programming languages has been virtually synonymous with the development of structuring. The earliest programming languages, which used primitive, unstructured lists, have been supplanted by modern, highly structured languages; and this trend still continues. Good structuring makes a program more readable, therefore easier to write and easier to debug. Thus it shortens the time required to design and maintain a program.

A Pascal program is made up of three main parts, each of which may contain several subparts:

1. Declarations.
2. Routines.
3. Main body.

Declarations serve two main purposes: They reserve some space within the memory of the computer where specific values of data will be stored, and they make it possible for the computer to check for syntactic errors within the program, thus making it more efficient and reliable.

A *routine* is a compact, readable unit containing a group of instructions that serve to accomplish a specific task. Two kinds of routines are used in Pascal: *functions* and *procedures.* Each function and each procedure is identified by a code name, by which we can call it up as often as needed in the program, without having to rewrite the instructions it contains.

Functions and procedures are the main tools used in writing programs. Usually, a program is made of a large collection of such routines, each carrying out a specific task. Together they accomplish the task of the program.

The *main body* of the program is a set of instructions that governs the overall execution of the program. In a program of significant size or complexity, the main body typically serves for "administrative" purposes, governing the sequence in which the routines are executed, while the actual computation is carried out in the routines. In a short program that executes a simple, single-purpose computation—like our line-drawing problem—there may be no need for special-purpose routines, and the main body may perform the actual computation.

Program DRAWLINE is an actual Pascal program that draws the line we discussed earlier. It is stored in a *file*, which is the basic "package" of information that computers handle.

This simple program can help us identify some of the basic characteristics of any Pascal program:

1. Every program has a header, which includes its name and, optionally, a list of control parameters in parentheses.
2. Comments may be placed anywhere in the program. They serve only to help the programmer understand the program; but are ignored by the computer. A comment is designated by the markers (* *) or { }.
3. The keywords BEGIN and END designate a block of code—a group of statements that are to be treated as one syntactical unit—within the main body or within a routine. Like parentheses in an arithmetical expression, blocks may be nested within one another.
4. Semicolons (;) *separate* statements in a Pascal program. Therefore, they are used only between different consecutive statements. You will notice that there is no semicolon after the LEAVEGRAPHICSMODE statement because it is not followed by another, different statement within its BEGIN-END block.
5. Blanks can appear almost anywhere in the program. A single blank is significant to the computer, for it serves to separate the words in a statement.

PROGRAM DRAWLINE

```
program drawline (output);
(* draws a line from screen location <100,200> to
   screen location <500,600> *)

   procedure entergraphicsmode; external;
   procedure leavegraphicsmode; external;
   procedure moveto (x,y : integer); external;
   procedure drawto (x,y : integer); external;

begin
   entergraphicsmode;

   moveto (100,200);
   drawto (500,600);

   leavegraphicsmode
end.  (* of drawline program *)
```

If several blanks occur together, the computer treats them as a single blank. We take advantage of this fact, using many blanks to *indent* lines in a way that will make the structure of the program apparent to the programmer.

6. The program as a whole is terminated by a period (.).

In the programs that are presented in this book, we will often use EXTERNAL routines like the four in Program DRAWLINE. The external procedure named ENTERGRAPHICSMODE puts the terminal in graphic mode and sets the speed of data transmission. LEAVEGRAPHICSMODE returns the terminal to alphanumeric mode. MOVETO moves the electron beam to the specified position without leaving a trace on the screen. DRAWTO moves the electron beam to the specified location, leaving a visible line as it goes.

As you can imagine, these routines are highly technical and specific to the particular display device that one uses. That is why they are "external"—so that every programmer does not have to be familiar with the technical details of every display device. Rather, one programmer who is an expert on a particular device writes and tests the routines to perform certain well-defined operations on that device. The routines are then placed in a *library,* which is available to all programmers.

When a library routine is needed in a program, we simply declare the name of the routine followed by the keyword EXTERNAL. This tells the compiler that the body of the routine is to be found "external" to the program—namely, in the library. The library must be loaded with the program after it has been compiled, and the two will execute as if they were a single program.

Certain operating systems, like UNIX (which was developed by AT&T's Bell Labs), make provisions to *include* such library routines within the code of the program itself, without actually copying them. In this book we will use that provision, to save space and to enhance clarity. The particular instruction that we will use is:

```
# include "drivers.i"
```

To see what the file DRIVERS.I contains, see Appendix B.

□ SUMMARY

The principal parts of a computer are:

1. The CPU, which interprets instructions, retrieves data from memory, and performs computations.
2. The memory units—the main memory, which stores data needed for the computation currently being performed; and the auxiliary memory, which provided long-term storage for masses of data.

3. The input/output device, by which the computer communicates with humans.

Programming comprises a chain of transformations that allow us to utilize a computer for purposeful problem solving. The programmer's tasks are:

1. To devise an *algorithm*—a step-by-step, unambiguous set of instructions for solving the problem.
2. To translate the instructions into a *high-level* programming language.

The computer's tasks are:

1. To *compile* the program, translating the high-level instructions into *assembly code* and that into binary *machine code*—the instructions that actually make the computer operate.
2. To execute the instructions, producing the result that the programmer specified.

Debugging involves iteration through the programming process, eliminating two kinds of errors:

1. Syntactical errors, which prevent the compiler from translating the high-level *source code* into low-level *object code*.
2. Logical errors, because of which the result that the programmer *specified* does not correspond to the result that he *intended*.

The main parts of a Pascal program are:

1. Declarations, which allocate space in memory for certain data and enable the compiler to check for syntactical errors.
2. Routines, such as functions and procedures, which contain the instructions to perform a specific task.
3. The main body, which governs the overall execution of the program.

2

NAMES

Chapter 1 described how, in principle, a computer works when it is instructed to draw a line: It performs some numerical computations and then channels the resulting values to an output device. In a similar way, the computer can follow a set of instructions that enable it to store and retrieve information from memory. This in turn enables the computer to perform still more elaborate computations. Now the question arises how does the computer (or, more precisely, the central processing unit) know which memory cells need to be accessed so that data can be retrieved from them or stored in them? In this chapter we will study these important kinds of transactions and how they are controlled by the programmer at the highest level.

□ MEMORY

The memory of a computer, as discussed earlier, is made of cells that contain one piece of information each. Each cell has a unique address so it can be identified and its content may be modified (within some constraints). Figure 2.1 is a stylized depiction of this arrangement, in the form of a chessboard.

Each square is identified by its sequential location in the ranks and files of the board, which acts as the square's "address space." The current "content" of the square is depicted by the chess piece that is stationed on it. Note that contents in many cases are not unique: There may be up to eight identical pawns of each color stationed on different squares, and two each of the bishops, knights, and rooks. As the game progresses, the content of each cell may change, but not its address. Figure 2.1 thus depicts a "snapshot" of the chess game at a particular point in time. We can call it the current *memory map* of the game, with the chess board acting as a 64-cell memory.

Analogously, the computer's memory is made of a very large number of cells—typically millions of cells—each with a unique address. The address of each cell is fixed for each computer but varies from one machine to the other.

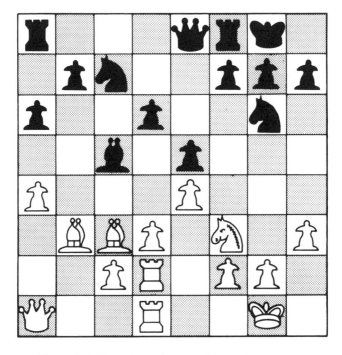

Figure 2.1. Chess board as a metaphor for memory.

The content of each cell, on the other hand, is variable. It may consist of a number, a character, an operation (such as +), or even the memory address of another cell.

☐ IDENTIFIERS

In our chess game example, it is easy enough for the players to identify the pieces and the operators that move them by specifying the respective rank and file numbers of their starting and resting squares. There are only 64 such positions. However, in the computer's memory, which has millions of memory cells, the programmer would have a formidable task in trying to keep track of the particular memory cells that contain pertinent data.

Furthermore, the programmer is not really interested in the actual memory address of the cells he uses. He only wants assurance that the correct cell will always be accessed when instructed. As a matter of fact, if the programmer were to specify actual memory locations, the program would become inseparably tied to the particular computer on which it was written. The program would thus lose the important quality of portability to other machines. When the computer becomes outdated and has to be replaced by a newer model, the effort expended in developing the software would be lost.

A solution to the problem of identifying memory cells at the high level of programming has been found by adopting conventions similar (but not identical) to those used in algebra, where symbols denote *variables* that may assume *different values* at different times. Applying this concept to computers, we identify particular cells by *name* rather than by their address in the memory. The computer associates each name with a particular physical memory location, and the name serves as an intermediary between the program and the hardware. There are two advantages to using names rather than physical memory addresses:

1. Names are chosen by the programmer, not the hardware manufacturer, making them easy to remember and manipulate.
2. Since the computer is now responsible for associating the names with physical memory location (an operation that occurs during the compilation phase), the program is no longer dependent upon a particular machine and can be transported to other computers when desired.

High-level programming languages, such as Pascal, allow the programmer to choose the names, which are called *identifiers,* according to the particular needs of the program. When the program is compiled, each identifier is automatically associated with a particular memory cell, thereby relieving the programmer from having to specify the actual cells where the information is now stored.

An identifier in Pascal can be any sequence of characters and numerals that complies with two simple rules:

1. It must begin with a letter.
2. It must not contain any blanks or punctuation marks.

Some legal identifiers that comply with these rules are

FRANK
WINDOW
X
A1
DECEMBER25
X1X

Some illegal identifiers that violate one or both rules are

2BY4
U.S.A.
FIRST OF APRIL
1X
JOHN DOE
24"

One further restriction is that some character sequences are reserved by the language for special purposes, and they cannot be used as identifiers. A full list of reserved words can be found in Appendix A.

□ VALUES

Values are the contents stored in memory cells. They may include numbers (both whole and fractions), characters, operators, and the memory address of other cells. For most practical purposes, programmers are concerned with only four basic types of values:

1. Integers (whole numbers)
2. Reals (decimal numbers)
3. Characters (letters, numerals, and symbols)
4. Booleans (the values TRUE and FALSE)

Operators are handled explicitly in the form of arithmetical *expressions*, while the addresses of other memory cells are handled indirectly through *pointers*, which we will discuss in later chapters.

An *expression* consists of one or more values that are combined by means of *operators*, such as the regular arithmetic operators:

+ (addition)
− (subtraction)
* (multiplication)
/ (division)

Expressions may also be parenthesized, in which case the order of their evaluation is dictated by the nesting of parentheses rather than by the normal precedence rules (multiplication and division before addition or subtraction). For example,

$$2*(3 - (4 + 4)) = -10$$

□ ASSIGNMENTS

How do we associate a value with an identifier? That is, how can the programmer explicitly instruct the computer to store a particular value in a memory cell that is identified by a particular symbol? The operator that assigns a value to a memory cell identified by some user-defined symbol is known as the *assignment operator*, and it is denoted by

: =

For example,

```
A  := 3.0;
B  := 3.8 + 5.7
```

The meaning of the assignment operator is as follows:

1. Evaluate the expression on the right-hand side of the assignment operator.
2. Then, store that value in the memory cell that is identified by the name on the left-hand side of the assignment operator.

This interpretation means that the assignment operator is characterized by having a single identifier on its left-hand side, and a value (or an expression that can be evaluated into such a value) on its right-hand side. Therefore, a statement such as

A + B := 5

is *illegal* since the left-hand side is not a single identifier.

The assignment operator thus *associates* a value with the name on its left-hand side. That value can later be retrieved and used in subsequent computations by simply mentioning that name. For example,

```
A  := 5;
B  := 6;
C  := A + B
```

After the last statement had been executed, the value associated with the name C is 11.

Since the expression on the right-hand side of the assignment operator is evaluated *before* it is assigned, it is possible (and often very useful) for the symbol appearing on the left-hand side to be used within the expression on the right-hand side. For example,

```
A  := 5;
A  := A + 1
```

After the last statement has been executed, the value stored in the memory cell identified by A is 6. This method allows us to increment (increase by 1) the value of some variables, a practice that is often used for counting the number of times some operation has taken place.

□ SUMMARY

In order to store and retrieve information, the computer puts one item of information in each cell of its *memory,* just as chess pieces are assigned to squares on the chessboard. The programmer assigns an identifying *name* to each memory cell he uses. The computer keeps track of the actual physical *address* that is associated with each name, where the information is to be found.

The information contained in a memory cell is called a *value*. A value may be a number (integer or real), a character, a boolean, an operator, or the address of another memory cell. A value is associated with an identifier by means of the *assignment operator.*

3

VALUES

We have seen the role of *identifiers* as a high-level names for specific memory cells, and how *values* can be associated with those names by means of the *assignment* operator. We now turn to the important issue of "rules," or constraints, that govern this process.

A number of problems would arise if there were no rules governing the assignment of values to names. The same would be true if there were no rules to the game of chess. Physically, chess pieces could be placed on any desired square of the chess board. However, this sort of unrestricted play would soon result in a meaningless jumble. To make the game meaningful, we impose certain restrictions as to which piece may occupy a certain square at any given time. For example, a white king may not occupy a square checked by a black piece.

Similarly, we impose restrictions on the type of values that may be associated with a particular name. Consider, for example, the following sequence of statements:

```
a := true;
b := 5;
c := a + b
```

The first statement assigns the value TRUE to the identifier A. TRUE is what we call a BOOLEAN value (we will learn more about such values later in this chapter). The second statement assigns the numerical value 5 to the identifier B. The problem arises in the third statement, which attempts to add the values associated with A and B.

How can we prevent such errors, which may pollute the memory with nonsense values and thereby render our computation meaningless? One way would be for the computer to test the values before an operation is performed on them and stop or inform the programmer if a potential error might arise. This method is, however, not satisfactory since it detects only the symptoms of a problem and

25

not the problem itself. Furthermore, once the program is running, there is nothing the programmer can do about this error, short of starting all over again.

The solution employed by Pascal is simple and effective. It consists of two parts:

1. Declare what type of values can be associated with each name (identifier).
2. Instruct the computer to verify that each expression that is assigned to that name results in a value of the appropriate type.

This way values will not be allowed to be associated with names of an inappropriate type, and the operations that use these names can be guaranteed "no-nonsense" values. This solution has two additional advantages:

1. It lets the computer know the names and the number of names that will be used throughout a particular computation, thus optimizing its memory management.
2. It can be done at compilation time, before the program is actually executed.

This second advantage is particularly important since it allows us to detect and correct a good deal of errors before we even start using the program, thereby increasing the program's reliability and saving much debugging time.

To implement this solution method, Pascal classifies values into four basic types:

1. Integers
2. Reals
3. Characters
4. Booleans

Values can only be associated with names of the appropriate type. Thus, for example, if A is designated to be associated with values of type integer, it can *only* be associated with values of type integer.

By knowing the type of the values in an expression, the computer may also test whether the operation about to be performed on them is meaningful. For example, it will not allow multiplication of two values of type character or of type boolean.

□ DECLARATIONS

Informing the computer of the type of values that each name may be associated with is performed in the *declarations* part of the program. Each identifier is declared to be of a certain *data type*. The data type associates each name with a set of possible values and operations. For example, the declarations:

```
var     x : real;
        y : integer;
        m : boolean;
        k : char;
```

will convey to the computer the following information:

1. X, Y, M, and K are VARiables. Thus values may be assigned to them, and the values may change in the course of the computation.
2. The variable X must be assigned REAL numbers only; the variable Y must be assigned INTEGER numbers only; the variable M must be assigned BOOLEAN values only; and the variable K, only CHARacters.
3. The *operations* that may be applied to a value identified by X are $+$, $-$, $/$, $*$, and some other operations associated with REAL numbers. Those that may be applied to a value identified by Y are $+$, $-$, $*$, and some other operations associated with INTEGER numbers. Those that may be applied to a value identified by M are the logical operators AND, OR, and NOT. Values identified by K may only be read, written, and compared to another value of the same type.

Once we have conveyed this information to the computer, it will allocate the appropriate memory cells for the variables, and from now on it will recognize the variables for what they are. If at some place in the program we use a variable called Z, which was not previously declared, the compiler will tell us that there is an error in the program. It will also check every occurrence of each declared variable in the program to see if it has been misused somehow, such as being assigned a wrong value:

```
m := 2
```

or having a *wrong operator* applied to it:

```
x := m + k
```

This service, known as *type checking*, trades freedom for rigor. First, we must declare all the variables before they can be used. If somewhere in the program we notice that we need another variable, it is not possible to "pull it out of the air." Rather, we must go back and declare it. Second, our freedom is restricted in assigning values to variables and in operating on them.

Most programming languages use type checking to enforce a well-formed code, but some do not. BLISS and GEDANKEN are such typeless languages. In these languages the programmer has great freedom, but must also assume the responsibility for assuring that the program will be meaningful by not mixing different values.

Syntax Rules

The syntax rules for declaring variables in the program are as follows:

1. The declaration part of a program must begin with the reserved word VAR (denoting it as a VARiables declaration block). Then comes the identifier (the name of the variable, which we choose); a colon (:); the type of this variable; and finally a semicolon (;), which is the common separator of Pascal statements. For example,

   ```
   var    x : real;
   ```

2. A number of variables, all of the same type, may be written together in the same statement, separated by commas. For example,

   ```
   var    x,w,z : real;
   ```

3. The declaration block may also contain many variables with different types, all having the same standard structure and all sharing a single VAR declaration. For example,

   ```
   var    x,w,z : real;
          y     : integer;
          a,b,c : boolean;
   ```

Note that expressions, like variables, have types as well as values. The type of an expression can be determined from the types of the elements within it, and it must match the type of the variable to which the value of the expression is assigned. For example, if we declare

```
var    value,start,step,count : integer;
```

we can then use these variables in the following way:

```
value := start + step*count
```

This expression uses integer operands and operations, so it is evaluated to an integer value. That value is then assigned to the variable called VALUE, which is also of type integer.

☐ LITERALS AND CONSTANTS

Before we define each one of the standard data types in Pascal, we should note that there are two other classes of values that are somewhat different from others. These are the literals and the constants.

Literals are simply values that are written in the program directly as they are, rather than being computed. For example, in the assignment

```
x := 2
```

the symbol 2 is a literal because it has the same value that it represents literally, namely the number 2.

However, if we do not wish to use the literal itself in a program (and there are good reasons why we should not), we may give it a name and instruct the computer that the value associated with that particular name should not be modified throughout the program (or part of it). In this case, the identifier we use for that value is known as a *constant.*

For example, when drawing a circle, it is convenient to use polar coordinates, which can be translated (as we shall see later) into cartesian coordinates through two simple trigonometric functions. When such a translation is performed we must first represent the angular location of points on the circle through radians, using the conversion factor 0.0174533:

```
angle := location*0.0174533
```

If we must repeat this statement many times it would be awkward (and a potential source of errors) to write the literal 0.0174533 (or was it 0.175433?) every time we need it. Since this quantity never changes, we may instead declare a constant that has the same value but a meaningful name, such as

```
const    radians = 0.0174533;
```

Now every time we need 0.0174533 we can use RADIANS instead.

The declaration of constants is similar to that of variables. It begins with the reserved word CONST, which is followed by an identifier, an equation sign, and a literal or another constant that has already been declared. For example,

```
const    biggest  = 1000;
         smallest = - biggest;
```

The CONST declaration block comes before VAR declarations block. Thus the constants may be used in the declaration of variables, as we shall see later.

Note that literals and constants also have types. For example, in

```
const    x = 3.14;
         y = 5;
```

X is of type REAL and Y is of type INTEGER. Their types are known implicitly from their content, so they do not have to be declared explicitly. Since each literal or constant is of a known type, it is subject to the same rules as a variable: it may be operated on only by certain operators, and it may be assigned only to certain variables. In addition to these restrictions, its value may not be modified.

Using Constants Instead of Literals

There are several good reasons for using constants rather than literals, and well-written programs rarely use literals outside the constant declaration block.

If a constant value has some meaning in the program, that meaning can often be reflected through a mnemonic identifier that makes the program easier to read and to understand than it would be if it were filled with "magical" numbers. The use of RADIANS instead of 0.0174533 is a good example.

In some cases the constant is actually a parameter of the particular application in which it is used. For example, suppose we wish to draw a circle on the CRT screen. Most CRTs are not capable of drawing a true circle, but can only approximate it by drawing a many-sided polygon. The number of sides of the polygon is up to the programmer, but for good results the programmer should know something about the CRT on which the circle is to be displayed. If the CRT is of low resolution, then it would be a waste of time to give the polygon too many sides, for the circle will appear somewhat rough anyhow. But if it is a high-resolution CRT, then we can take advantage of that fact by giving the polygon a large number of sides to make a very smooth approximation of a circle.

If we initially write the circle-drawing routine for a low-resolution CRT, we could specify the number of sides with a literal such as 24. But later on we might wish to upgrade the program for a high-resolution CRT. We would then have to search the code for the number 24, which might appear in several different places. By this time we may have forgotten that the literal 24 stood for resolution. And there might be some occurrence of the literal 24 that has nothing to do with resolution, which may get changed inadvertently, causing disastrous results.

It would be much safer, and the code would be a lot more readable, if we defined the resolution with a constant instead of a literal in the first place:

```
const    resolution = 24;
```

This way we need to change only a single well-defined value in order to increase the resolution when we upgrade the hardware.

☐ STANDARD DATA TYPES

In Pascal there are four standard data types that may be used in the VAR declaration block. These are INTEGER, REAL, BOOLEAN, and CHAR. We shall examine each of these types and the operators that are associated with them in the following sections.

Integer

Integers are whole numbers that may be positive or negative. Zero is an integer, and so are 63 and -25. However, 1.5 and 2.71 are not integers. Variables of type INTEGER can be declared in the VAR declaration block in the following manner:

```
var     i,j  :  integer;
```

and can be assigned values such as

```
i  :=    5;
j  :=  -13
```

There is a physical upper bound on the memory of the computer, which is due to the finiteness of the hardware. Therefore we can only use some finite subset of the mathematically infinite set of integers. For any particular computer there is an integer called MAXINT, and every integer N that we use must therefore be within the range:

$$-\text{MAXINT} <= N <= \text{MAXINT}$$

An attempt to evaluate an expression whose value is outside this range will lead to a run-time error. For most practical purposes, however, we can regard the set of integers on the computer in the same manner as the mathematical integers.

The operators that may be applied to integers are

$$+ \quad - \quad * \quad \text{DIV} \quad \text{MOD}$$

with the standard precedence rules of multiplication and division performed before addition and subtraction.

These are all *infix* operators, which means that they are written between their operands, as in conventional algebra. The operator $-$ may also be used as a *unary* operator, as in -50.

The operators $+$, $-$, and $*$ represent addition, subtraction, and multiplication, respectively. For example,

```
i  :=  2  +  3*4  -  28
```

The usual division operator $/$ is not defined for integers because, unlike $+$, $-$, and $*$, the division of two integers may yield a real number. For example,

$$3/2 = 1.5$$

If X, Y, and Z were declared as integer variables, the following expression would be illegal:

```
x := y / z
```

To overcome this shortcoming, pascal provides two other operators that perform parts of the division operation. These are the DIV and MOD operators. DIV yields an integer by ignoring the remainder. MOD yields an integer by ignoring everything but the remainder or *modulus* of the number. For example,

$$5 \text{ DIV } 2 = 2 \qquad 2 \text{ DIV } 5 = 0$$
$$5 \text{ MOD } 2 = 1 \qquad 2 \text{ MOD } 5 = 2$$

As an example of these nonintuitive operators, consider Program MIXED-UNITS, which converts a distance from inches to yards, feet, and inches; for example, 67 inches = 1 yard, 2 feet, and 7 inches.

PROGRAM MIXEDUNITS

```
program mixedunits (output);
(* co verts inches to mixed units of yards, feet,
   and inches *)

   const    yard = 36;
            foot = 12;

   var      length,yards,feet,
            inches,remainder  : integer;

begin
   (* get length typed by user *)
   readln(length);

   (* compute how many yards are in length *)
   yards := length div yard;

   (* how many inches are left? *)
   remainder := length mod yard;

   (* compute how many feet are in the remainder *)
   feet := remainder div foot;

   (* how many inches are left? *)
   inches := remainder mod foot;

   write (yards:3, feet:3, inches:3)
end.  (* of mixedunits program *)
```

In addition to these infix operators, there are also some predefined or "built-in" functions in Pascal:

PRED, SUCC, ABS, and SQR

Each of these functions takes an integer *argument*—that is, the value of the parenthesized expression, which is passed to the function, and yields an integer value. The function PRED yields the predecessor of its argument, and SUCC yield the successor. For example,

```
PRED(5)  =  4
SUCC(-3) = -2
```

ABS yields the absolute value of its argument, and SQR its square:

```
ABS(10)  = 10    SQR(10)  = 100
ABS(-10) = 10    SQR(-10) = 100
ABS(0)   =  0    SQR(0)   =  0
```

Note that SQRT (the square root operator) is not defined for integers for the same reason that / (the division operator) is not defined for them: it might yield a result of type REAL.

Reals

Reals are numbers that contain a decimal point: 2.7, 0.3, 5.0, and so on. Note that the decimal point must always be preceded and followed by a numeral; thus we must write "0.3" instead of ".3" and "5.0" instead of "5.". Variables of type REAL can be declared in the VAR declaration block in the following manner:

```
var     r,s : real;
```

and can be assigned values such as

```
r := 2.7;
s := 3.14
```

As with integers, the computer can represent only a finite subset of the mathematically infinite set of reals, but for practical purposes we may usually ignore this fact. What we may not ignore, and which is a major deficiency of the representation of real numbers in the computer, is their finite precision. Every computer can represent only a finite number of significant digits after the decimal point. For example, the irrational number PI (while theoretically infinitely long) will be truncated to something like PI = 3.1415926535. An expression such as

$$(1 - X)/(1 + X)$$

may produce invalid results for very small values of X, such as $X = 0.00001$, because for most practical purposes the computer will consider 1.000001 equal to 0.99999. This may not seem like much of a difference, but a repeated operation on such imprecise values, or using them in multiplications (or divisions) with greater numbers, will cause the error to grow rapidly. If we have a sequence of operations such as

```
y := (1 - x)/(1 + x);
z := 1/(1 - y)
```

we may get a run-time error for dividing by zero if the value of X is small. This is an example of a problem known as round-off errors.

The limited precision of real numbers also means that we must refrain from basing tests on comparisons of two real numbers; that is, we must not instruct the computer to perform some operation until some predefined real value has been reached. For example,

```
x := 0.7;
repeat
  x := x + x
until x = 2.8
```

This iteration may never halt even though 2.8 is theoretically within the range of X because it is based on strict equality. If X should be evaluated to 2.799999 rather than 2.8, the equality would not hold.

Scientific Notation. Another way to write real numbers in Pascal is by *scientific notation*—the representation of a number as a multiple of a power of 10:

$$
\begin{aligned}
378.5 &= 3.785E2 \\
-34.1 &= -3.41E1 \\
0.341 &= 3.41E-1
\end{aligned}
$$

This representation is particularly convenient for very large or very small numbers, such as the rest mass of an electron, which is

0.00000000000000000000000000910956 grams

or

9.10956E-28

Operators. The operators that may be applied to reals are $+$, $-$, $*$, and $/$. Additional standard functions that are provided for use with reals are TRUNC and ROUND, which transform a real into an integer. TRUNC does it by throwing away all the digits after the decimal point, and ROUND does it by rounding the real number into the closest integer. For example,

TRUNC(3.14) = 3   ROUND(3.14) = 3
TRUNC(2.7) = 2   ROUND(2.7) = 3

Other standard functions that may be used on reals are

ABS   (absolute)
SQR   (square)
SQRT   (square root)
SIN   (sine)
COS   (cosine)
ARCTAN   (arctangent)
LN   (natural logarithm)
EXP   (exponent) that for EXP(R) returns the irrational number e raised to the power R.

Each of these standard functions yields a real value. Note that ABS and SQR work for integers too; they return an integer if the argument is an integer and a real if the argument is a real.

Coercion. Integer values may be used in expressions of type REAL; that is, they may be assigned to a variable of type REAL. They will thus be transformed into reals. If one operand of any of the operators $+$, $-$, or $*$ is of type REAL, then the rest of the operands are automatically transformed into reals. This transformation is known as *coercion*. The coercion will take place before the operator is applied and before the expression as a whole is evaluated. For example,

$(6 + 4)*(1 + 0.1) = 11.0$

Note that the result is a number of type REAL, even though in this case it has an integer value.

The operator / (division) coerces both its operands to be reals, and the result is real, as we saw earlier.

Equality of REAL Numbers. We stated earlier that due to numerical imprecision, values of type REAL cannot be tested for strict equality. But some sort of test of equality is often needed. How can we overcome this problem? One simple way is to define some very small real number (such as $1E - 6$) as a constant called EPSILON. Two real values X and Y can be assumed to be equal if

```
abs(x - y) < epsilon
```

Characters

A variable of type CHAR has a value that is a character. This includes the set of all lowercase and uppercase letters, digits, and blanks, special symbols (such as &, *, +, −), and some symbols that cannot be printed (such as carriage return and escape).

A literal of type CHAR is a character that is enclosed in single quotes, for example,

'A' represents the letter A, and
' ' represents a blank

Variables of type CHAR can be declared in the VAR declaration block in the following manner:

```
var     c,d : char;
```

and can be assigned a value such as

```
c := 'a';
d := 'z'
```

Operators. The operations on variables of type CHAR include only comparisons, for example,

is C = D?

Here we try to match the values previously stored in the two variables C and D, so that the comparison results in

is 'A' = 'Z'?

In addition to strict equality, the set of characters is ordered: 'B' is "greater than" 'A' but "less than" 'C', and so on:

'A' < 'B' < 'C' < ... < 'Z'

Thus we may use all the relational operators:

<   (less than),
<=   (less than or equal to),
<>   (not equals),
>   (greater than),
>=   (greater than or equal to)

with variables of type CHAR; the comparison yields a value of type BOOLEAN.

The following are standard functions that may be applied to variables of type CHAR, exploiting the fact that CHARs are ordered:

ORD(C) yields the position of the character in the list of all available characters (its ordinal number).

CHR(N), the inverse of ORD, yields the character whose ordinal number is N. (N must be a positive integer in the range 0 through 127.) This is a particularly convenient feature of Pascal, used when we need to "send" to the computer an unprintable character (such as ESCAPE, which is very common in graphic applications).

PRED(C) yields the character preceding the argument C.

SUCC(C) yields the character succeeding the argument C.

Figure 3.1 lists all the printable characters in their ordinal values, corresponding to the ASCII code (American Standard Character Information Interchange).

ORD	CHR	ORD	CHR	ORD	CHR	ORD	CHR	ORD	CHR
32 =	' '	52 =	'4'	72 =	'H'	92 =	'\'	112 =	'p'
33 =	'!'	53 =	'5'	73 =	'I'	93 =	']'	113 =	'q'
34 =	' " '	54 =	'6'	74 =	'J'	94 =	'^'	114 =	'r'
35 =	'#'	55 =	'7'	75 =	'K'	95 =	'−'	115 =	's'
36 =	'$'	56 =	'8'	76 =	'L'	96 =	' ' '	116 =	't'
37 =	'%'	57 =	'9'	77 =	'M'	97 =	'a'	117 =	'u'
38 =	'&'	58 =	':'	78 =	'N'	98 =	'b'	118 =	'v'
39 =	' ' '	59 =	';'	79 =	'O'	99 =	'c'	119 =	'w'
40 =	'('	60 =	'<'	80 =	'P'	100 =	'd'	120 =	'x'
41 =	')'	61 =	'='	81 =	'Q'	101 =	'e'	121 =	'y'
42 =	'*'	62 =	'>'	82 =	'R'	102 =	'f'	122 =	'z'
43 =	'+'	63 =	'?'	83 =	'S'	103 =	'g'	123 =	'('
44 =	','	64 =	'@'	84 =	'T'	104 =	'h'	124 =	'|'
45 =	'-'	65 =	'A'	85 =	'U'	105 =	'i'	125 =	')'
46 =	'.'	66 =	'B'	86 =	'V'	106 =	'j'	126 =	'~'
47 =	'/'	67 =	'C'	87 =	'W'	107 =	'k'	127 =	' '
48 =	'0'	68 =	'D'	88 =	'X'	108 =	'l'		
49 =	'1'	69 =	'E'	89 =	'Y'	109 =	'm'		
50 =	'2'	70 =	'F'	90 =	'Z'	110 =	'n'		
51 =	'3'	71 =	'G'	91 =	'['	111 =	'o'		

Figure 3.1. ASCII characters.

Using Figure 3.1, it is easy to verify the following equalities:

```
CHR(43)   = '+'
ORD('+') = 43
ORD('A') = 65
ORD('2') = 50 (note: ORD('2') is not 2!)
```

Booleans

The data type BOOLEAN has only two values:

TRUE and FALSE

The words TRUE and FALSE may be used as boolean literals. However, their use is mostly limited to initialization of boolean variables, since it is not normally necessary to use them in the boolean expressions themselves. Variables of type BOOLEAN can be declared in the VAR declaration block in the following manner:

```
var    t,f : boolean;
```

and can be assigned values such as

```
t := true;
f := false
```

As we shall see later, booleans are used primarily in conjunction with control statements that effect the sequence in which the statements of a program are executed, and arise as a result of comparing expressions. They are named after George Boole, the nineteenth-century mathematician who developed much of the theory of logic.

Operators. There are three operators that may be used with boolean operands:

AND
OR
NOT

If we declare

```
var    finished,empty,toobig : boolean;
```

then the following expressions have boolean values (true or false), depending on the individual values of the variables they use:

```
finished and empty or toobig
not empty or toobig
toobig and (empty or finished)
```

The precedence of these logical operators is as follows:

1. The operator NOT is always applied first. For example,

```
not empty or toobig = (not empty) or toobig
```

2. The operator AND is always applied before OR. For example,

```
finished and empty or toobig =
(finished and empty) or toobig
```

In addition to the boolean operators, there are relational (comparison) operators that may be applied to expressions of any type on which ordering has been defined, and whose application yields a boolean value. These operators are:

$=$	(equals)	$5 = 4$	is FALSE
		$421 = 421$	is TRUE
$<>$	(not equal)	$5 <> 4$	is TRUE
		$421 <> 421$	is FALSE
$<$	(less than)	$5 < 4$	is FALSE
		$421.1 < 422.2$	is TRUE
$>$	(greater than)	$5 > 4$	is TRUE
		$421.1 > 422.2$	is FALSE
$<=$	(less than or equal to)	$421 \leq 422$	is TRUE
		$422 \leq 421$	is FALSE
$>=$	(greater than or equal to)	$421 \geq 422$	is FALSE
		$422 \geq 421$	is TRUE

One standard function that may be assigned to boolean variables is

```
odd(x)
```

It yields the value TRUE if the integer expression X has an odd value, and FALSE if it has an even value.

The value of a boolean expression may be assigned to a boolean variable. For example, if we declare

```
const    maximum  = 1000;

var      finished : boolean;
         counter  : integer;
```

we can then write expressions such as

```
finished := counter > maximum
```

Logical Expressions. A simple boolean expression consists of a series of boolean values combined through AND, OR, and NOT. For example,

((A AND B) OR C) AND (NOT D)

However, when we compose expressions with more than one boolean operator, we must be able to accurately analyze their composite value (meaning). Consider Program LOGIC.

What are the values of VALUE1, VALUE2, and VALUE3? To help us in evaluating such expressions, we use *truth tables*. Like addition and multiplication tables, truth tables represent all the possible combinations of the values TRUE and FALSE through the boolean operators AND, OR, and NOT:

AND	T	F
T	T	F
F	F	F

OR	T	F
T	T	T
F	T	F

NOT	
T	F
F	T

Truth tables are read in the following way: Find the value of the left operand among the row headers and the value of the right operand among the column headers, then find the value of the expression as a whole at the table entry corresponding to that row and column.

PROGRAM LOGIC

```
program logic (output);

var     finished,empty,toobig : boolean;
        value1,value2,value3  : boolean;

begin
  finished := true;
  empty := false;
  toobig := true;

  value1 := finished and empty or toobig;
  value2 := not empty or toobig;
  value3 := toobig and (empty or finished);

  write (value1:7, value2:7, value3:7)
end.  (* of logic program *)
```

All logical expressions consist of simple arguments combined through operators and parentheses. Once we know the values of the constituent arguments we can determine the value of the entire expression by consulting the truth tables, keeping in mind the precedence of operations.

We can now evaluate VALUE1, VALUE2, and VALUE3:

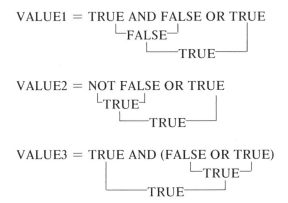

The ability to evaluate logical expressions correctly is particularly important for correct termination of loops, and for choosing between two possible courses of action, as we shall see in the next chapter.

☐ SUMMARY

In order to make a meaningful program, we must follow certain rules in assigning values to names. In Pascal, we must inform the computer what type of values may be associated with each name that we intend to use. Pascal will then check that every value assigned to each name is of the appropriate type. It will also check that every operation applied to a value is permissible for that type.

The *declaration* part of a program contains a list of the names of all *variables* to be used, specifying the *data type* for each variable. *Constants* must also be declared, but their type is known implicitly and is not specified. *Literals* are values that are written out explicitly in the program, rather than using a symbolic name; they are not declared at all.

Pascal provides four standard data types: INTEGER, REAL, CHAR, and BOOLEAN.

INTEGERs are whole numbers (positive or negative). Hardware limitations restrict the value of integers to some number MAXINT, which is different for each computer. The operators that may be applied to integers are + (addition), − (subtraction), * (multiplication), DIV (integer division), and MOD (modulus, or remainder of division). Also, integers may be operated on by the functions PRED (predecessor), SUCC (successor), ABS (absolute value), and SQR (square).

REALs are numbers that contain a decimal point. Hardware limitations restrict the precision of real numbers; we cannot test two reals for strict equality for there may be some rounding error due to the limits of precision. The operators that may be applied to reals are $+$, $-$, $*$, and $/$ (division). A real may be reduced to an integer by the functions TRUNC and ROUND. Also, reals may be operated on by ABS, SQR, and SQRT (square root); the trigonometric functions SIN, COS, and ARCTAN; and the logarithmic functions LN and EXP. An integer may be substituted into a real expression; it is then *coerced* to a real.

CHARacters are letters, digits, and symbols. They may be operated on only by comparisons. Since the characters have a value based on their order in the ASCII table of characters, they may be compared as $=$ (equals), $>$ (greater than, i.e., later in the list), $<$ (less than, or earlier in the list), or some combination of these operators. Characters may also be operated on by the functions ORD (ordinal number), CHR (inverse of ORD), PRED, and SUCC.

BOOLEANs have the values TRUE and FALSE. The operators that may be applied to booleans are AND, OR, and NOT. A logical expression is a series of boolean values combined through these operators; its value can be determined with the aid of *truth tables*.

4

EXERCISE 1

The following Program TRIANGLE draws a triangle on the screen of a graphic terminal, if it is loaded and executed with the appropriate drivers (see Appendix B). The endpoints of the triangle are at ⟨100,100⟩, ⟨700,100⟩, and ⟨400,500⟩, in screen coordinates. Each side of the triangle is drawn by assigning the appropriate values to the variables named X and Y, respectively, then either "moving to" the designated location (without drawing a visible line), or "drawing to" that location (while showing the line).

Note that the value assigned to Y in the first DRAWTO command was not modified by the second DRAWTO command (why?)!

Using this example as reference, write a program that generates a picture on the screen. The nature and complexity of the picture are up to you, but they should provide evidence of your understanding the process.

PROGRAM TRIANGLE

```
program triangle (output);
(* draws a triangle on the screen *)

# include "drivers.i"

var     x,y : integer;

begin
  entergraphicsmode;

  x := 100;   y := 100;   moveto (x,y);
  x := 700;               drawto (x,y);
  x := 400;   y := 500;   drawto (x,y);
  x := 100;   y := 100;   drawto (x,y);

  leavegraphicsmode
end.  (* of triangle program *)
```

PART TWO

CONTROL

5

REPETITION

In Chapter 4 we saw how we could draw a picture on the screen of a graphic display terminal by specifying in the body of a program all the points and lines that make up the drawing. If we did not like the result, we had to edit the program and rerun it. This is a rather limited and nonintuitive way of producing drawings, and it is unsuitable for complex drafting work. In more realistic settings we want to have control over the process of drawing in real time; that is, to be able to influence directly what is drawn on the screen without having to determine beforehand what will be drawn, and without having to use explicit coordinate values to make our intentions clear to the computer. We call such capabilities *control*. In order to exercise control over an executing program, the user (in our case, the designer)—rather than the programmer—must have the means to convey instructions to the program, and the program must have the means to accept and interpret them.

The process of conveying instructions to a program while it is executing is known as interaction. *Interaction* is a dialog between the user and the program. The user issues a command that the computer interprets and responds to accordingly. The user may issue another command, that in turn is interpreted and executed by the computer, and so on until the task is accomplished.

In graphic systems we can provide interaction capabilities by employing an input device called a *cursor*. The cursor is a means to point at an arbitrary location on the screen and have the coordinate values of that point registered by the computer. The location of the cursor on the screen is typically marked by a cross hair or a blinking cross so that the precise point the user is indicating can be seen. The computer can "sense" this location and translate it into a pair of X,Y coordinates. Physically, the cursor can be driven by a joystick, a pair of thumb wheels, a stylus on a graphic digitizing tablet, cursor control buttons, a mouse, or many other devices.

For the purposes of this book, cursor location and registration are provided to the program by the routine READCURSORLOCATION(X,Y). Its action is the inverse of the routines DRAWTO(X,Y) and MOVETO(X,Y), which we have already encountered. Rather than place a mark on the screen at the location of coordinates ⟨X,Y⟩, it retrieves the ⟨X,Y⟩ screen coordinates where a marker (the cursor) is positioned. When the program encounters the statement READ-CURSORLOCATION(X,Y) the computer turns on the cursor, allows the user to move it about the screen until the desired screen location is found, and waits for the user to make some action indicating that this location is to be registered (typically by pressing RETURN or another keyboard key, or by pressing a button on the pointing device).

A very simple implementation of cursor control and registration, demonstrated in Program DRAW1, waits for the user to position the cursor and register its location.

The results of executing this program and registering the location of the cursor somewhere on the screen are shown in Figure 5.1.

The cursor is, then, a simple device that can be utilized to convey to the program dynamically the location of any point on the screen that is of interest to the user.

The ability to interact with a program is, however, not sufficient by itself to exert control; the program must have the means to interpret commands and use the data to perform actions. These require two important classes of programming constructs:

1. Repetition constructs
2. Branching constructs

PROGRAM DRAW1

```
program draw1 (input,output);
(* draws a line from the lower-left corner of the
   screen to a user-indicated screen location *)

# include "drivers.i"

var x,y : integer;

begin
  entergraphicsmode;

  readcursorlocation (x,y);
  drawto (x,y);

  leavegraphicsmode
end.  (* of draw1 program *)
```

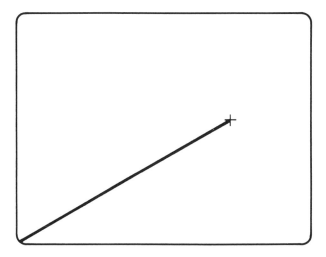

Figure 5.1. Positioning the cursor on the screen.

Repetition constructs allow us to capture within a finite number of lines in the program a potentially infinite process, such as designing a house. *Branching* constructs allow the program to choose between alternative actions, as directed by the user or by the results of some computation.

In the following sections we will discuss these issues in detail and their particular implementation in Pascal.

□ LOOPING CONSTRUCTS

A drafting system that is capable of drawing only one line, even if its endpoints are interactively definable by the user, is of very little practical value. To be useful at all, the system must at least be capable of drawing multiple lines. In other words, the sequence of operations

```
readcursorlocation(x,y);
drawto(x,y);
```

demonstrated in Program DRAW1 must be repeated. With each repetition, the program will allow the user to position and register the location of the cursor, and it will draw a line to that point from the previously registered location of the cursor, as depicted by Figure 5.2.

Repetition is a very important concept in programming because it allows us to execute the *same statements* in a program over and over again with *different sets of data.* In the above example, the statements that we want repeated include only

```
readcursorlocation(x,y);
```

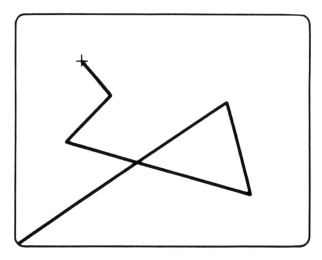

Figure 5.2. Drawing multiple connected lines.

and

```
drawto(x,y);
```

These two statements never change. However, the data they operate on, namely the X,Y coordinates, is constantly modified by the user through the indication of various points on the screen. The coordinates of these points constitute the data that the two statements operate on, and are associated with the variables X and Y. The content of these cells changes every time the user repositions and registers the cursor. Each time their content is used by the two statements, different actions occur: Different lines are drawn on the screen.

Pascal provides the programmer with several tools to perform such repetition, called *looping constructs*. Each of them includes two important ingredients:

1. A directive to *repeat* the execution of a group of statements several times.
2. A *termination* condition that, when evaluated to TRUE (or FALSE, in some cases), will cause the repetition to cease.

How can the user indicate the desire to terminate the repetition of the line-drawing sequence? The principle we shall use to direct the nature of operations is based on designating some region of the screen with a special meaning. If the cursor location is registered within that region, it will signal the program that the user wishes to control its execution in some predefined way. For example, it may indicate that the user wishes to terminate the line-drawing loop. Obviously, it is not sufficient just to designate some region of the screen as having a special meaning, but the position of the cursor must actually be tested during each iteration through the loop to see if it has been registered within that region, and if it had—the looping must be terminated.

Let us assume, for example, that the top 10 percent of the screen has been designated as the "loop termination area." In other words, if the registration of the cursor yields a point whose Y value is greater than 700, then the line-drawing loop should be terminated. To make this special screen region apparent to the user, so the loop will not be terminated inadvertently, we can draw a line at the boundary between the general drawing area on the screen (the lower 90 percent) and the loop termination area (the top 10 percent), as depicted in Figure 5.3.

Partitioning the screen into two areas with different meanings is very significant. The lower part has become the *drawing area,* where the user creates a picture, while the upper part has become the *loop termination area,* which does not affect the picture itself, in the sense of adding more lines to it, but rather affects the *process* by which the picture is generated. Obviously, the program must be made to recognize the different meanings and respond accordingly.

Pascal provides us with three looping constructs that are basically variations of the same concept of repetition and termination. Each construct can be replaced by another construct, perhaps less efficiently, but nevertheless the computational power is exactly the same: No one of the three constructs can do anything that the other two cannot. The three looping constructs are called the REPEAT-UNTIL loop, the WHILE loop, and the FOR loop.

The REPEAT-UNTIL Loop

This control structure repeats the execution of a group of statements until some condition is fulfilled. It uses the keywords REPEAT and UNTIL to group to-

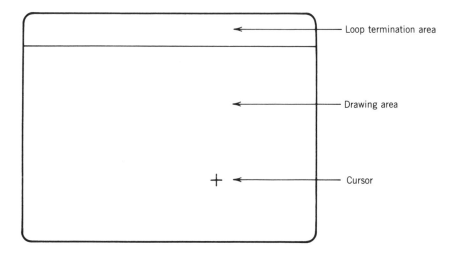

Figure 5.3. Designating a portion of the screen as the loop termination area.

gether the statements to be repeated so that several statements, separated by semicolons, can be executed repeatedly. These statements constitute the *body* of the loop.

In our example of drawing multiple line segments interactively, the RE-PEAT-UNTIL loop could be used in conjunction with screen partitioning, as demonstrated in Program DRAW2.

Program DRAW2 also demonstrates some other important features of the REPEAT-UNTIL looping construct. It shows that the general form of the loop structure is

>REPEAT
>>statement;
>>statement;
>>.
>>.
>>.
>>statement
>UNTIL condition;

PROGRAM DRAW2

```
program draw2 (input,output);
(* draws multiple connected line segments to user-
    indicated screen locations *)

# include "drivers.i"

var   x,y     : integer;

begin
  entergraphicsmode;

  (* draw dividing line between loop termination
     area and general drawing area *)
  moveto (0,700);   drawto (1000,700);

  (* position cursor at origin *)
  moveto (0,0);

  (* draw *)
  repeat
    readcursorlocation (x,y);
    drawto (x,y)
  until y > 700;

  leavegraphicsmode
end.  (* of draw2 program *)
```

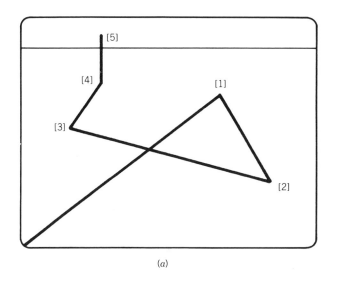

(a)

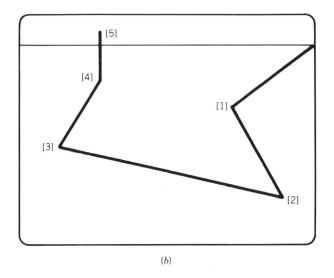

(b)

Figure 5.4. Results of the loop in Program DRAW2.

The statements constitute the body of the loop, and the condition—which is a logical expression—causes its termination when it evaluates to TRUE.

Particular attention must be paid to the following properties of the looping construct:

1. Initial conditions
2. Termination condition
3. Sequence of statements in the body of the loop

The initial conditions that are set before entering the loop may have profound effects on the results. In Program DRAW2, the statement MOVETO(0,0) causes the first segment to be drawn from the origin of the screen coordinate system rather than from the end of the boundary line between the two screen areas, which happens to be the last position of the cursor before entering the loop. Figure 5.4 shows the different results of drawing to the same five points in the same order when the statement MOVETO(0,0) is removed.

The statements that constitute the body of the loop must have an effect on the termination condition, so it will eventually be satisfied; otherwise the loop will continue to iterate forever. In Program DRAW2, READCURSORLOCA-TION(X,Y) causes a change in the value of Y, as well as that of X. When the cursor is registered in the loop termination area its Y value is indeed larger than 700, causing the logical expression at the end of the loop to evaluate to TRUE and thereby terminate the loop.

The order of the statements inside the body of the loop may also have profound consequences on the resulting computation. In the above example, only two statements make up the body of the loop. Switching them so that DRAW-TO(X,Y) occurs before READCURSORLOCATION(X,Y) will have the following effect: The program will *not* draw the last line segment, connecting the point that was used to terminate the operation (inside the loop termination area) with the rest of the drawing. Such results may be desirable if we wish to contain the drawing in the drawing area, reserving the screen area above the boundary line for control purposes only.

A *side effect* of switching the order of DRAWTO(X,Y) and READCUR-SORLOCATION(X,Y) is that the program will draw a very short line (a point, really) to location ⟨0,0⟩ where the command MOVETO(0,0) positioned the cursor just before entering the loop. A side effect may not have any adverse effects, as in this case; but it should be accounted for since in later applications it may have significant consequences for the drawing.

The WHILE Loop

Our second looping construct is called the WHILE loop. It allows the program to execute a group of statements *while* some condition is true. This loop has the general form:

```
WHILE condition DO
    BEGIN
        Statement;
        Statement;
        .
        .
        Statement
    END;
```

This looping construct is demonstrated in Program DRAW3, which is very similar to DRAW2.

The WHILE loop differs significantly from the REPEAT-UNTIL loop. One difference is apparent in program DRAW3: we had to add the pair of keywords BEGIN-END around the statements that constitute the body of the loop to indicate that they belong to a group that will be repeated as a whole. Without this grouping, only the first statement will be repeated. Thus the effect of BEGIN-END on a group of statements is similar to that of parentheses on the symbols of an arithmetical expression: It renders the group a *block* of statements that can be treated as one unit. Such BEGIN-END grouping was not required in the REPEAT-UNTIL loop because the loop structure itself provided the necessary grouping statements, thereby defining the extent of the repeating group.

Another significant difference is that the WHILE and the REPEAT-UNTIL looping constructs evaluate the condition in different places. In the REPEAT-UNTIL loop the condition is evaluated *after* the group of statements is executed, whereas in the WHILE loop it is evaluated *before* the statements are executed. This means that the body of a REPEAT-UNTIL loop will be executed *at least once,* even if the condition is TRUE the first time through. The body of a WHILE loop, however, will not be executed at all if the condition is FALSE to begin with.

It is interesting to note in this context that the REPEAT-UNTIL loop operates under a FALSE-valued condition and terminates when the condition becomes TRUE, whereas the WHILE loop operates under a TRUE-valued condition and terminates when the condition becomes FALSE.

A third difference concerns the initialization of the variables that are used in the condition that terminates the loop. These variables must be identified and correctly initialized. In the WHILE loop they must have a well-defined value upon entering the loop, but in the REPEAT-UNTIL loop they may be assigned values within the body of the loop itself. It is for this reason that the assignment

```
y := 0;
```

has been added before the body of the loop. Without it, the program will be unable to evaluate the logical expression in the WHILE statement the first time it encounters it because Y will have no value at all.

PROGRAM DRAW3

```
program draw3 (input,output);
(* draws multiple connected line segments to user-
   indicated screen locations *)

# include "drivers.i"

var   x,y      : integer;

begin
  entergraphicsmode;

  (* draw dividing line between loop termination
     area and general drawing area *)
  moveto(0,700); drawto(1000,700);

  (* position cursor at origin *)
  moveto(0,0);

  (* initialize y so the loop will execute *)
  y := 0;

  (* draw *)
  while y <= 700 do
    begin
      readcursorlocation(x,y);
      drawto(x,y)
    end;

    leavegraphicsmode
end.  (* of draw3 program *)
```

In order to decide whether to use the WHILE or the REPEAT-UNTIL loop-ing construct, we must consider all the above points. In particular, we must de-termine whether the body of the loop should be executed at least once or whether there may be a case in which it should not be executed at all.

The FOR Loop

Many times when we want to execute a statement repeatedly, the number of repetitions is known in advance and does not depend on the effect of statements within the loop. Pascal provides the programmer with a looping construct for just such a case. This construct is called the FOR loop. It executes the body of the loop a predefined number of times, using a variable called the *loop control variable* to count the number of iterations.

We can use the FOR loop to write a program that draws an approximated circle. By using only DRAWTO commands we cannot draw a smooth circle. We can, however, approximate it by drawing many very short lines each of whose endpoint coordinates satisfy the equation:

$$(X - CX)^2 + (Y - CY)^2 = R^2$$

where CX and CY denote the coordinate values of the center of the circle, and R denotes its radius, as depicted in Figure 5.5.

It is easy to assure compliance with this equation if we use polar coordinates to locate the endpoints of the segments through the parametric functions:

```
x := cx + r*cos(theta);
y := cy + r*sin(theta)
```

THETA is a parameter that denotes the incremented angle we use to locate the endpoint of each short line segment about the center. The circle-drawing program is described in Program CIRCLE1.

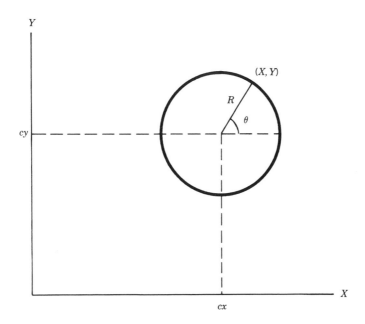

Figure 5.5. Computing point coordinates to draw an approximated circle.

PROGRAM CIRCLE1

```
program circle1 (output);
(* draws   an   approximated  circle   centered   at
   screen   location   <200,300>, which  has  a  radius
   of 100 pixels. the circle is approximated by 72
   straight   short   line   segments whose endpoints
   are computed through polar coordinates. *)

# include "drivers.i"

const   radians        = 0.0174533; (* conv. fac *)
        radius         = 100;
        cx             = 200;
        cy             = 300;
        approximation = 72;

var     i,x,y          : integer;
        theta          : real;

begin
  entergraphicsmode;

  (* move cursor to starting point *)
  moveto ((radius + cx), cy);

  for i := 1 to approximation do
    begin
      (* compute polar coords of next point *)
      theta := (i*360/approximation)*radians;
      x := cx + round(radius*cos(theta));
      y := cy + round(radius*sin(theta));

      drawto (x,y)    (* draw line segment *)
    end;

  leavegraphicsmode
end.  (* of circle1 program *)
```

The FOR loop, as shown in Program CIRCLE1, has the following form:

```
FOR loop_control_variable : =
     first_integer_expression TO second_integer_expression DO
   BEGIN
     statement;
     statement;
       .
       .
       .
   END;
```

The two integer expressions in the FOR loop statement determine the range within which the loop control variable will change: It starts by being assigned the value of the first expression and steps through the integers until it reaches the value of the second expression.

We can translate this process into a REPEAT-UNTIL or a WHILE loop that has the same effect:

```
loop_control_variable : =first_integer_expression;
WHILE loop_control_variable < =second_integer_expression DO
   BEGIN
     statement;
     statement;
       .
       .
       .
     statement;
     loop_control_variable : =loop_control_variable + 1
   END;
```

Program CIRCLE2 demonstrates the use of a WHILE loop to perform the same operation as did CIRCLE1.

Like the WHILE loop, the FOR loop may never execute if the second integer expression is smaller than the first one because the value of the loop control variable must be increased up to the value of the second integer expression. We could, instead, *decrease* its value by replacing the keyword TO with DOWNTO. This is analogous to replacing the < = sign (less than or equal to) in the WHILE loop with a > = sign (greater than or equal to) and *decrementing* the loop control variable instead of incrementing it.

The statements that comprise the body of the FOR loop are *not permitted* to affect its control variable. The reason for this is that the FOR loop contains an "automatic" increment or decrement mechanism, and tampering with the value

PROGRAM CIRCLE2

```
program circle2 (output);
(* draws   an   approximated   circle   centered   at
   screen   location   <200,300>,  which  has  a  radius
   of 100 pixels. the circle is approximated by 72
   straight   short   line   segments  whose  endpoints
   are computed through polar coordinates. *)

# include "drivers.i"

const   radians         = 0.0174533; (* conv. fac *)
        radius          = 100;
        cx              = 200;
        cy              = 300;
        approximation   = 72;

var     i,x,y           : integer;
        theta           : real;

begin
  entergraphicsmode;

  (* move cursor to starting point *)
  moveto ((radius + cx), cy);

  i := 1;   (* initialize loop counter *)

  while i <= approximation do
    begin
      (* compute polar coords of next point *)
      theta := (i*360/approximation)*radians;
      x := cx + round(radius*cos(theta));
      y := cy + round(radius*sin(theta));

      drawto (x,y);   (* draw line segment *)

      i := i + 1
    end;

  leavegraphicsmode
end.  (* of circle2 program *)
```

of the control variable would contradict the original purpose of this looping construct, which is to perform a predefined number of repetitions.

The FOR loop statement is therefore the "safest" looping construct in terms of termination: It is guaranteed to stop after a finite, predefined number of repetitions. It can never "run away," which is a prevailing risk in the other two looping constructs. The FOR loop is also clearer to the human reader since the number of iterations is explicit.

Nested Loops

In Pascal, each control structure forms a single statement. Thus it is possible to include any one as part of another. In particular, any one of the statements within the body of a loop may itself be a loop. This makes it possible to use *nested loops*—that is, to perform repetitions within repetitions.

For example, the circle-drawing program (CIRCLE1) can be made interactive, thereby allowing the user to draw many circles of different sizes and place them anywhere on the screen. We can do so by nesting the loop that draws a circle within the loop through which the user controls the action taken by the program. To allow for circles of various sizes, we shall require the user to specify two points. The first point denotes the screen location of the center of a circle; the second point, in conjunction with the first, will be used to calculate the radius of the circle. This interactive circle-drawing method is shown in Program CIRCLE3.

Note that in Program CIRCLE3 we use CY, the vertical screen location of the center, rather than the variable Y (which is one of the two endpoint coordinates of each line segment on the circle) as terminator for the user interaction. Other-

PROGRAM CIRCLE3

```
program circle3 (input,output);
(* draws  an approximated circle whose center and
   radius  are  determined  interactively  by the
   user.the circle is approximated by 72 straight
   short   line   segments  whose  endpoints  are
   computed through polar coordinates. *)

# include "drivers.i"

const   radians      = 0.0174533; (* conv. fac *)
        approximation = 72;

var     i,x,y         : integer;
        radius, cx,cy : integer;
        theta         : real;
```

```
begin
  entergraphicsmode;

  (* draw dividing line between loop-termination
     area and drawing area *)
  moveto (0,700);   drawto (1000,700);

  readcursorlocation(cx,cy);     (* center point *)

  while cy <= 700 do        (* main control loop *)
    begin
      readcursorlocation(x,y);  (* second point *)

      (* compute radius *)
      radius := round(sqrt(sqr(cx - x)
                        + sqr(cy - y)));

      (* move cursor to starting point *)
      moveto ((radius + cx), cy);

      (* draw circle *)
      for i := 1 to approximation do
        begin
          theta := (i*360/approximation)*radians;
          x := cx + round(radius*cos(theta));
          y := cy + round(radius*sin(theta));

          drawto (x,y)      (* draw line segment *)
        end;            (* of circle-drawing loop *)

      readcursorlocation(cx,cy)    (* new center *)
    end;              (* of main control looop *)

  leavegraphicsmode
end.  (* of circle3 program *)
```

wise the program might terminate prematurely, for the internal loop changes the value of Y somewhat independently of user control, and it might assign to it a value larger than 700 while drawing a circle, as depicted in Figure 5.6. Furthermore, we have used *three* READCURSORLOCATION commands: one outside the main loop, and two inside it. This was done in order to evaluate CY *before* each iteration so that the loop will terminate "cleanly" as soon as CY > 700, without drawing an extra circle in the loop termination area.

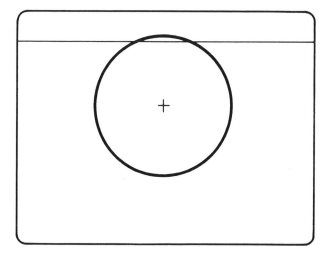

Figure 5.6. A circle crossing the boundary line.

☐ SUMMARY

In order to make a practical computer drafting system, we must let the user exert *control* over the program while it is executing. *Interaction* is a dialog between the user and the computer in which the user manipulates a *cursor* to inform the computer of locations and operations to be performed.

The user can interact with the computer through a series of actions controlled by a *looping construct*. Pascal provides three such constructs; all three have essentially the same powers, and all three contain a way to *repeat* an action and a way to *terminate* the loop.

The REPEAT-UNTIL loop executes a group of statements, known as the *body* of the loop, at least once. It then evaluates a *condition;* if the condition is FALSE, then the body is repeated, and the condition is tested again, and so on until the condition is TRUE.

The WHILE loop first tests a condition. If it is FALSE, then the body is not executed at all. If the condition is TRUE, then the body is executed, and the condition is tested again, and so on until the condition is FALSE.

The FOR loop does not test a condition, but rather has a built-in counter called a *loop control variable*. The body of the loop is executed for a predetermined number of times.

When using looping constructs, we must always be careful to check the initial values of the control variables, the nature of the termination condition, and the sequence of statements in the body of the loop. Otherwise the loop might continue forever, or it might produce undesired results.

We can *nest* a looping construct within another looping construct to build a more complex and powerful control structure.

6

BRANCHING

In Chapter 5 we studied how the user can control the location of lines and circles and how he can terminate the execution of the program as a whole. The lines he could draw were, however, connected; there was no way to start a new sequence of line segments disconnected from the rest. The reason for this deficiency was that once the loop was entered, it kept on performing DRAWTOs until it terminated. The user had no way of directing the computer to MOVETO the new cursor location instead of DRAWTO it, which would have started a new sequence of line segments. How can we tell the computer to perform a MOVETO instead of a DRAWTO—or for that matter, how can we instruct the program to choose between any two different actions while it is executing?

The answer, as before, lies in two provisions: a means to inform the computer of our wish and a means for the program to interpret the command. This chapter deals with the interpretation of commands through a programming construct called *branching*.

Before we begin our discussion of branching, let us first consider how we inform the computer of our choice of action. We can switch from action A to action B (in this case, from DRAWTO to MOVETO) by using the same method we used for terminating the drawing sequence as a whole: that is, designate an area of the screen as the *mode-switching* area.

Let us then designate the bottom 10 percent of the screen as the mode-switching area and mark its boundary with a line, as depicted in Figure 6.1. By registering the cursor location within that area the user can tell the computer to start a new line through a MOVETO operation. Having solved the user interface problem, we can now deal with the programming aspects: How will the program be able to interpret the mode-switching directive?

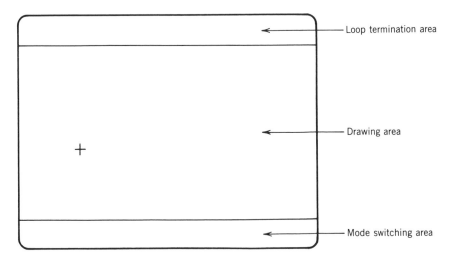

Figure 6.1. Screen partitioning with mode-switching area.

□ THE IF STATEMENT

For the purpose of switching modes, we can use a conditional evaluation construct known as the IF statement. This statement evaluates a logical expression and then executes one statement if its value is TRUE or another if its value is FALSE. For example,

```
if y < 70
   then newline := true
   else newline := false;
```

In this example the logical expression Y < 70 is enclosed between the two keywords IF and THEN. When evaluated, it yields one of two values, TRUE or FALSE, depending on the location of the cursor on the screen. If it evaluates to TRUE, the statement following THEN will be executed (NEWLINE := TRUE); otherwise the statement following ELSE will be executed (NEWLINE := FALSE). The ELSE clause of the IF statement may be omitted, in which case no action will be taken if the condition evaluates to FALSE; instead, the statement immediately following the IF statement in the program will be executed. Note that there are no semicolons before the THEN and before the ELSE clauses because the entire construct constitutes a single statement in Pascal.

We can now embed this construct in an interaction loop, thereby deriving a program that provides the user with the ability to draw lines, start new lines, and terminate execution at will. This program is DRAW4.

PROGRAM DRAW4

```
program draw4 (input,output);
(* draws user controlled multiple disconnected
   lines made of multiple connected segments *)

# include "drivers.i"

var   x,y     : integer;
      newline : boolean;

begin
  entergraphicsmode;

  (* draw upper and lower dividing lines *)
  moveto (0,700);   drawto (1000,700);
  moveto (0, 70);   drawto (1000, 70);

  (* initialize to "moveto" mode *)
  newline := true;

  (* draw lines interactively *)
  repeat
    (* get first user input *)
    readcursorlocation(x,y);

    (* perform drawing action *)
    if newline
      then moveto(x,y)
      else drawto(x,y);

    (* set mode for next action *)
    if y < 70
      then newline := true
      else newline := false
  until y > 700;

  leavegraphicsmode
end.   (* of draw4 program *)
```

Program DRAW4 contains two IF statements. The first affects the drawing directly; it determines whether the program performs a MOVETO or a DRAWTO. The second IF statement sets the value of the boolean variable NEWLINE that controls the first statement. We need this double structure to delay the effect of registering the cursor in the mode-switching area so that it will cause the *next* cursor registration point to become the starting point of a new line. Otherwise, the point of registration within the mode-switching area itself would become the starting point of a new line. The program thus must carry out two decisions, one of which is made directly by the user and the other one indirectly. Also note that NEWLINE, which is a variable of type BOOLEAN, need not be compared to TRUE in order to be evaluated: Its own value (either TRUE or FALSE) determines the outcome of executing the first IF statement.

The boolean variable NEWLINE is initialized to TRUE outside the loop. Without initialization, it would have no value the first time it is encountered inside the loop, and the result of its evaluation would be unpredictable. Its initialization to TRUE eliminates the need to move the cursor to the origin, as we did in Program DRAW3. Instead, the first cursor registration is presumed to be the beginning point of the first line.

Program DRAW4 allows the user to draw multiple disconnected lines. However, the last point of each line will be located either in the mode-switching area or in the loop termination area, as depicted in Figure 6.2.

This undesirable effect results from performing the DRAWTO directive regardless of the location of the cursor. There is no discrimination between cursor positioning for commands and cursor positioning for supplying data. It is easy, however, to correct this situation. We must simply test whether the cursor is in the drawing area before performing either a DRAWTO or a MOVETO and act accordingly. To do so all we need is to extend the logical expression in the first IF statement as follows:

```
if newline or (y > 700) or (y < 70)
   then moveto (x,y)
   else drawto (x,y);
```

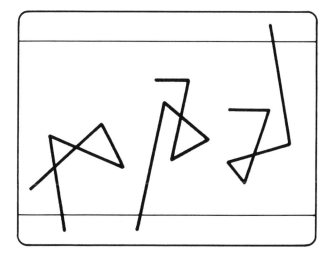

Figure 6.2. Drawing multiple disconnected lines.

This construct will perform a MOVETO not only when NEWLINE is TRUE but also if the cursor is outside the drawing area.

Multiple Choices

In Chapter 5 we learned how to draw circles as well as lines. We were, nevertheless, restricted to drawing one kind of figure only—either lines or circles. In the first part of this chapter we have introduced the concept of choice between two different courses of action, such as between DRAWTO and MOVETO. It would be very useful if we could also choose between drawing lines and circles within the same program. Logically, the user must then choose between three possible actions at each iterative step:

1. Draw a circle or draw a line.
2. If line drawing was chosen, the user must choose between:
   2.1. Starting a new line by means of MOVETO; or
   2.2. Continue adding segments to an existing line by means of DRAWTO.

Implementation of this hierarchical sequence of decisions relies on the typical two components of control: (1) the appropriate user interface and (2) structuring the program to interpret the commands appropriately.

For the user interface, we could designate another area of the screen as a "circle-drawing mode" area, where cursor registration will have the effect of switching from line-drawing to circle-drawing mode.

But we have already used up 10 percent of the screen for the loop termination area and another 10 percent of the screen for the mode-switching area. If we keep designating more control areas, before long there will be little space left for the drawing itself which is, after all, the purpose of the program.

Fortunately, the control areas need not take up so much space. All we are really after is some kind of a "button" to be pushed by registering the cursor. So we could reduce the size of the control areas and locate all of them somewhere where they will least interfere with the drawing itself.

In fact, it would be very effective to carry the button analogy even further, supplying the user with virtual buttons on the screen that will not only allow the user to select a desired action but also present all the possible actions that may be chosen. We call these buttons a *menu* since their purpose is similar to a menu in a restaurant, which tells the diner what courses are available for selection.

Figure 6.3 depicts a possible menu layout for our purposes that contains three boxes:

1. Newline
2. Circle
3. Quit

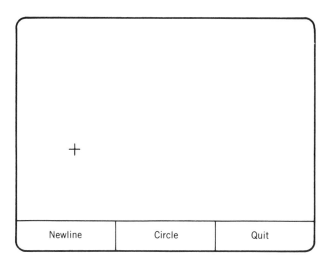

Figure 6.3. Screen menu buttons.

We shall see later how we can label the boxes to make their function more apparent to the user.

The user can choose any menu item by registering the cursor inside the corresponding box. But how will the program know which one of the boxes was selected?

The answer lies again in evaluating the X and Y locations of the cursor. The algorithm is as follows:

1. Is the cursor in the menu boxes area at all?
2. If so, is it in the NEWLINE box?
3. If not, is it in the CIRCLE box?
4. If not, it must be in the QUIT box!

If the answer to the first question is *no*, then the cursor must be within the drawing area of the screen, and the action that was previously selected prevails. If the answer to the first question is *yes* but the answers to the subsequent questions are *no*, then by default the cursor must be in the QUIT box.

Let us assume that the menu boxes occupy the bottom 10 percent of the screen, the left-most box ending at $X = 350$ and the right-most box starting at $X = 700$. The sequence of statements to determine the location of the cursor then becomes

```
if y < 70
  then if x < 350
          then newline := true
          else if x < 700
                  then circle := true
                  else quit := true
```

This sequence uses three boolean variables: NEWLINE, CIRCLE, and QUIT. Note that Y is evaluated only once, to determine whether the cursor has been registered in the menu area at all. If the value of Y is greater than (or equal to) 70, then the cursor was not in the menu area. In this case none of the subsequent IF statements will be executed, and the program will return to the beginning of the loop. But if the value of Y is less than 70, then the first evaluation of X will be performed. This test determines if X is less than 350, which means that NEWLINE has been selected. If this test fails, the program must still determine if the cursor has been registered in the middle box, which means that CIRCLE mode was selected. If this test too fails, then by default the cursor must be in the QUIT box.

Note that every THEN has a matching ELSE except for the first one. The indentation used in laying out the program makes it easier for the reader to recognize the matching THEN and ELSE clauses. The computer, however, requires no such aids to match them correctly. It always matches the ELSE clause to the last unmatched THEN, just as we match parentheses: The closing parenthesis always matches the last open one.

For the program to work properly, the variables that are used in this compound control structure must be assigned proper initial values. The *mode* of operation is initialized by setting NEWLINE to TRUE and CIRCLE to FALSE, so that the user will be able to draw a new line right from the beginning. We ensure that the program will not terminate prematurely by setting QUIT to FALSE before entering the loop. Program MENU1 implements these ideas.

This rather long program demonstrates some important principles of programming in general, and of good user interface in particular. The statements following both THEN and ELSE in the main IF statement have been expanded into COMPOUND statements—that is, statements that contain more than one command each. This was done by means of large BEGIN-END blocks, each consisting of a list of statements that together accomplish one task. Nested within the second block is another compound statement, the circle drawing block, which contains the necessary steps to determine the radius of a circle and draw it on the screen.

The main REPEAT-UNTIL control loop contains two major parts represented by the THEN and the ELSE clause of the outermost IF statement. The first clause determines which action should be taken, by testing the location of the cursor in the menu boxes or the drawing area. This information is then passed to the second clause of the outermost IF statement by means of the three boolean variables CIRCLE, NEWLINE, and QUIT. The second clause of this IF statement is the one that actually performs the desired action. Again we see the delay of one iteration cycle between determining the course of action and its execution. This delay is made explicit by the test that is performed by the outermost IF statement (IF Y < 70), which ensures that no lines or circles will be drawn when the cursor registers a menu selection. For example, when the user selects QUIT, no line will be drawn.

The initialization of the boolean control variables NEWLINE to TRUE and CIRCLE to FALSE after the circle has been drawn ensures that the program will let the user select a desired action at each iteration, rather than "get stuck" in one mode or another. Each time he wishes to draw a circle or start a new line, he must explicitly select that mode by registering the cursor in the appropriate menu box. The only *default* mode is continuous-line drawing by means of DRAWTO, so that line segments can be added without requiring intermediate command processing.

By *default* we mean an action that the program will take *unless* the user explicitly chooses another action. When designing a user interface, it is a good practice to have defaults whenever possible, so that the user does not have to make an explicit choice for every single action. Obviously, the default action should always be a *reasonable* action under the circumstances.

How do we know what action is reasonable? Making DRAWTO the default action is a good example of this decision. We could easily have chosen CIRCLE DRAWING to be the default mode, or MOVETO; but we chose DRAWTO instead. This choice allows a user to add segments to a new line without having to issue intermediate commands, which is a rather natural way of drafting. It is not unreasonable to require the user to indicate a change of mode in order to draw a circle or start a new line, but continuous-line drawing is really a single mode.

Defaults, unfortunately, are not always this easy to choose, and experimentation with prototypes may be necessary before a final decision is made.

☐ THE CASE STATEMENT

Program MENU1 demonstrated the use of multiple choices, which is one of the most common practices in interactive CAD systems.

However, the proliferation of THEN-ELSE clauses is cumbersome and is therefore a potential source of errors. To alleviate this situation Pascal provides another programming construct, called the CASE statement, which facilitates multiple choices. The CASE statement is a generalization of the IF statement, enabling the program to execute one of several possible actions depending on the value of a single variable. It reduces the number of tests that need to be performed to determine the appropriate course of action, and it makes the program more readable.

PROGRAM MENU1

```
program menu1 (input,output);
(* draws multiple disconnected lines and circles,
   selectable interactively by the user *)

# include "drivers.i"

const   radians                 = 0.0174533;
        approx                  = 72;

var     cx,cy,i,radius,x,y  : integer;
        circle,newline,quit : boolean;
        theta,r,angle,dx,dy : real;

begin
  entergraphicsmode;

  (* draw menu box lines *)
  moveto (0,70);        drawto (1000,70);
  moveto (350,70);      drawto ( 350, 0);
  moveto (700,70);      drawto ( 700, 0);

  (* initialize mode control variables *)
  quit    := false;
  circle  := false;
  newline := true;

  repeat                    (* user interaction loop *)
    readcursorlocation (x,y);        (* get input *)

    if y < 70         (* test if it is a command *)
      then begin              (* parse command *)
            if x < 350
              then newline := true
              else if x < 700
                    then circle := true
                    else quit := true
          end
      else begin              (* execute command *)
            if circle
              then begin        (* draw circle *)
                    (* center point *)
                    cx := x;   cy := y;

                    (* get second point *)
                    readcursorlocation (x,y);
```

```
                          (* compute radius *)
                          r := sqrt(sqr(cx-x) +
                                    sqr(cy-y));
                          radius := round(r);

                          (* draw circle *)
                          moveto ((cx + radius), cy);

                          for i := 1 to approx do
                            begin
                              angle := i*360/approx;
                              theta := angle*radians;

                              dx := radius*cos(theta);
                              dy := radius*sin(theta);

                              x := cx + round(dx);
                              y := cy + round(dy);

                              drawto (x,y)
                            end;

                          (* turn off circle mode *)
                          circle := false;

                          (* turn on newline mode *)
                          newline := true
                        end (* of circle drawing *)

                else if newline  (* line drawing *)
                        then   begin
                                 moveto (x,y);
                                 newline := false
                               end
                        else   drawto (x,y)
          end           (* command execution part *)

   until quit;   (* end of user interaction loop *)

   leavegraphicsmode
end.   (* of menu1 program *)
```

The general form of the CASE statement is

CASE expression OF
    constant-1 : statement;
    constant-2 : statement;
    .
    .
    .
    END;

PROGRAM MENU2

```
program menu2 (input,output);
(* draws multiple disconnected lines and circles,
   selectable interactively by the user *)

# include "drivers.i"

const    radians              = 0.0174533;
         approx               = 72;

var      cx,cy,i,radius,x,y  : integer;
         mode                : integer;
         theta,r,angle,dx,dy : real;

begin
  entergraphicsmode;

  (* draw menu box lines *)
  moveto (0,70);        drawto (1000,70);
  moveto (350,70);      drawto ( 350, 0);
  moveto (700,70);      drawto ( 700, 0);

  (* initialize mode control variable *)
  mode := 2;                   (* newline *)

  repeat                 (* user interaction loop *)
    readcursorlocation (x,y);        (* get input *)

    if y < 70        (* test if it is a command *)
      then begin                 (* parse command *)
           if x < 350
             then mode := 2            (* newline *)
             else if x < 700
                     then mode := 1  (* circle *)
                     else mode := 4    (* quit *)
           end
```

```
    else case mode of        (* execute command *)
         1 : begin              (* draw circle *)
               (* center point *)
               cx := x;    cy := y;

               (* get second point *)
               readcursorlocation (x,y);

               (* compute radius  *)
               r := sqrt(sqr(cx - x) +
                         sqr(cy - y));
               radius := round(r);

               (* draw circle *)
               moveto ((cx + radius), cy);

               for i := 1 to approx do
                 begin
                   angle := i*360/approx;
                   theta := angle*radians;

                   dx := radius*cos(theta);
                   dy := radius*sin(theta);

                   x := cx + round(dx);
                   y := cy + round(dy);

                   drawto (x,y)
                 end;

               (* set mode to newline *)
               mode := 2
             end; (* of circle drawing part *)

         2 : begin     (* line drawing part *)
               moveto (x,y);

               (* set mode to draw line *)
               mode := 3
             end;
         3 : drawto (x,y);      (* draw line *)
         4 : ;                  (* quit *)
       end     (* of command execution part *)

  until mode = 4;    (* end of user interaction *)

  leavegraphicsmode
end.  (* of menu2 program *)
```

The expression following the keyword CASE is evaluated to a constant value, which is matched against the constant values following OF. Only the statement following the matched constant will be executed; all the others are ignored. The constants must all be of the same type. Often INTEGER is used; but we will see that an enumerated type may also be used. A constant of type REAL should not, however, be used because of the precision problems that were discussed earlier. There should be no two constants with the same value, and exactly one of the values should match that of the expression. If the same action is to be executed for more than one constant, all these constants can be put on the same choice line, separated by commas. If one of the choices requires no action at all, a blank statement (containing only a semicolon) can be used.

Program MENU2 demonstrates the use of a CASE statement. It replaces the three boolean control variables of Program MENU1 (NEWLINE, CIRCLE, and QUIT) with a single integer variable, called MODE. Note how this replacement makes the program as a whole more readable and eliminates the need for multiple initializations. The only initialization that remains is MODE:=2, which sets it to MOVETO. We will assume that MODE = 1 means draw a circle, MODE = 2 means start a new line, MODE = 3 means add a segment to an existing line (DRAWTO), and MODE = 4 means quit.

Selecting a CASE statement instead of multiple IF statements is somewhat similar to selecting a FOR loop rather than a REPEAT-UNTIL or a WHILE loop, as discussed in Chapter 5. The CASE statement has no more computational power than multiple IF statements have, but it presents clearly the options that the data may assume and the corresponding actions. It can only be used when the values of the control data are known in advance, as in Program MENU2 where the variable MODE could only assume one of four predefined values. Just as the FOR loop is preferred over the REPEAT-UNTIL and WHILE loops, the CASE statement is preferred over multiple IF statements whenever it can be used.

□ SUMMARY

To choose between two different actions, we must provide a way for the user to inform the program of his choice and a way for the program to interpret the choice.

The user interface can be accomplished by providing a mode-switching area on the screen. As choices proliferate, we can condense all the choices into one region of the screen, with a small virtual button for each choice, which together make a menu of all possible actions.

Interpreting the user's choice can be accomplished by the IF statement or by the CASE statement.

The IF statement evaluates a logical expression. If the expression is TRUE, then the statement following THEN is executed. If the expression is FALSE, then the statement following ELSE (if there is an ELSE clause) is executed. Both the THEN clause and the ELSE clause may contain another IF-THEN-ELSE statement, and this nesting may repeat any number of times, creating a complex decision structure.

The CASE statement is a simpler way of presenting a complex decision structure, provided that all the possible values of some expression are known. The CASE statement evaluates this expression and matches it against the values listed after the keyword OF. When a match is found, the corresponding action is executed.

7

PARTITIONING

The last program we studied, MENU2, is an example of a program becoming increasingly complex as we add features. In truth, MENU2 is still a relatively simple program; it allows the user to choose only between line-drawing mode and a circle-drawing mode. Consider how complicated it may become when we add features enabling the user to select rectangles, triangles, or any predefined shape. And when we let the user define shapes dynamically instead of relying on those predefined by the programmer. You can see that, to be truly useful for CAD, a program may quickly become very complex indeed. As the program proliferates with variables and nested control statements, and as it increases in sheer size, it may far exceed our capabilities to keep it tractable and manageable—that is, unless we use some methodical way to curb and contain its ever-growing complexity.

The principles we employ for this purpose are called *abstraction* and *partitioning*. Abstraction and partitioning are processes for collecting all the relevant details that support a single concept into one package that can be likened to a labeled "box." By encapsulating different parts of the program in such packages, we can effectively partition the program into units or modules that can operate in harmony without one having to be concerned with the internal workings of another.

Abstraction and partitioning are the hallmarks of a hierarchical design process, whereby the overall features of the designed artifact are laid out first and the interactions between them carefully specified. Later, each functional unit may be further developed and detailed; the only constraint is to comply with the previously defined interface to other units. In designing a building, it is common to start with mass studies and space allocations. Later, the materials that enclose the spaces can be specified, along with building details, color, and texture. Using these principles, the architect can deal with relatively few concepts at a time. Otherwise he would be overwhelmed by the abundance of details that need to be attended to when designing even a simple building.

The principles of abstraction and partitioning apply equally to the design of a computer program. When we examine Program MENU2 in light of these principles, we can readily identify several different functional units. They include:

1. Drawing the lines that define the menu boxes.
2. Getting and parsing the commands issued by the user (identifying which menu box, if any, was selected).
3. Drawing circles.
4. Drawing lines.

It would greatly simplify the design and maintenance of the program if these units could be isolated and dealt with independently. Suppose we find a better way to parse user commands. Modularity will make it easy to replace the current method with the new, improved one without affecting any of the other modules that make up the program.

☐ PROCEDURES

Pascal provides us with the tools to exercise abstraction and partitioning through a *procedural* abstraction mechanism. Using these tools, the programmer can define his own computational modules and refer to them by name.

The use of the procedural abstraction mechanism is easily demonstrated by an example far removed from programming: baking a cake. Most cook books separate the preparation of the icing from the preparation of the cake itself since the same icing (say, chocolate fudge) may be used with different cakes (butter cake, toasted butter pecan, etc.). Rather than repeat the specifications every time the icing is to be used, the books describe it once it great detail and from then on refer to it by name.

The cake-icing example demonstrates another programming practice facilitated by the procedural abstraction mechanism: It often happens that a particular set of actions needs to be executed several times in a program. We may avoid writing out the Pascal statements every time they are required by defining them to be a *procedure,* and giving them a name. This set of operations may then be *invoked* by simply referring to that name.

To demonstrate this concept, let us consider two programs—RECTANGLES1 and RECTANGLES2—that draw a screen full of rectangles. Program RECTANGLES1 does not use procedural abstraction, while Program RECTANGLES2 does. Both programs have exactly the same result, as shown in Figure 7.1. However, Program RECTANGLES1 treats the actual drawing of each rectangle at the same level of abstraction as it treats the loop that controls their screen location.

Program RECTANGLES2, by contrast, separates the drawing of a single rectangle from the control structure that governs its location on the screen. This

separation makes the program more readable and thus easier to modify and
maintain. For example, we could easily have substituted Procedure DRAW-
RECTANGLE with a procedure called DRAWCIRCLE that draws, as its name
implies, circles instead of rectangles (provided its body has been set up to do so).
The result would have been a screen full of circles instead of rectangles, with only
one minor change to the program itself.

Before we apply the procedural abstraction mechanism to MENU2, thereby
making it clearer and ready for further expansion, let us consider the syntactical
issues of using procedural abstraction in Pascal.

PROGRAM RECTANGLES1

```
program rectangles1 (output);
(* draws screen full of rectangles *)

# include "drivers.i"

const   width = 100;   height =  80;
        dx    = 120;   dy     = 100;
        nx    =   8;   ny     =   8;

var     i,j,x,y : integer;

begin
   entergraphicsmode;

   x := 10;               (* leftmost starting point *)

   for i := 1 to nx do       (* number of columns *)
      begin
        y := 10;          (* lowermost stating point *)

        for j := 1 to ny do       (* number of rows *)
           begin                   (* draw rectangle *)
             moveto (x,y);
             drawto (x,(y + height));
             drawto ((x + width),(y + height));
             drawto ((x + width),y);
             drawto (x,y);

             y := y + dy            (* move up one row *)
           end; (* for j *)

        x := x + d       (* move right one column *)
      end; (* for i *)

   leavegraphicsmode
end. (* of rectangles1 program *)
```

PROGRAM RECTANGLES2

```
program rectangles2 (output);
(* draws screen full of rectangles *)

# include "drivers.i"

const    dx = 120;    dy = 100;
         nx =   8;    ny =   8;

var      i,j,x,y : integer;

  procedure drawrectangle (r,s : integer);
  (* draws a rectangle whose lower-left corner is
     at <r,s> *)

  const    width = 100;    height =  80;

  begin
    moveto (r, s);
    drawto (r, (s + height));
    drawto ((r + width), (s + height));
    drawto ((r + width), s);
    drawto (r, s)
  end; (* of drawrectangle procedure *)


begin (* main program *)
  entergraphicsmode;
  x := 10;              (* leftmost starting point *)

  for i := 1 to nx do       (* number of columns *)
    begin
      y := 10;        (* lowermost stating point *)

      for j := 1 to ny do      (* number of rows *)
        begin
          drawrectangle (x,y);

          y := y + dy           (* move up one row *)
        end;  (* for j *)

      x := x + dx       (* move right one column *)
    end;  (* for i *)

  leavegraphicsmode
end.  (* of rectangles2 program *)
```

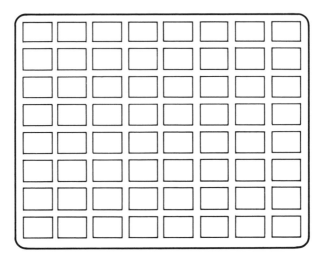

Figure 7.1. A screen full of rectangles.

Declaring and Calling Procedures

When using procedures, we must provide two things: a declaration of the proce-dure and its invocation. The procedure is declared after the VAR declaration block (i.e., before the main program). It is similar in structure to the Pascal program as a whole, as we have seen so far, in that it has a header, a declarations block, and a body that consists of statements; these parts can be seen in Progam RECTANGLES2. The header

```
procedure drawrectangle (r,s : integer);
```

is composed of three elements: the keyword PROCEDURE; the identifier DRAWRECTANGLE, by which this procedure will be known; and a parenthe-sized list of variables, with their type declarations. These variables are called the *parameters* of the procedure. They act as an interface, or gateway, between the body of the procedure and its environment, passing information in and out.

The declarations block also specifies the constants and the variables that are to be used *inside* the procedure. In this case we use only two constants, WIDTH and HEIGHT. These are followed by a BEGIN-END block of statements, which comprise the body of the procedure. Note that this block ends with a semicolon, like any other Pascal statement that is followed by other statements.

The procedure is called, or invoked, in the main program by writing its name, followed by a parenthesized list of variables or constants:

```
drawrectangle(x,y);
```

The variables listed in parentheses following the name of the procedure are called the *arguments* of the procedure. Each argument corresponds to one parameter in the procedure declaration; thus X corresponds to R, and Y corresponds to S.

We will discuss the properties of the parameters in more detail later in this chapter. Let us first consider how the procedural abstraction mechanism works by itself, let alone communicate with its environment.

How Do Procedures Work?

When the execution of the main program encounters a procedure call, it transfers control over to the procedure's body and executes it. When the procedure finishes executing, control returns to the main program, beginning at the statement following the procedure call. Just as the main program can call procedures, procedures can call procedures. These are known as *nested calls*. In a nested call, the program repeats the control transfer mechanism in the same way as before, always returning to the statement following the last call, as depicted in Figure 7.2.

Scope Rules

Typically, as in Program RECTANGLES2, procedures contain not only statements but also declarations of variables and constants. Such internal declarations raise three questions:

1. What is the "life span," or scope, of variables and constants declared inside the procedure? In other words, can we use these declared items after we have left the procedure and control has returned to the calling environment?

2. Are variables declared outside the body of the procedure also "visible" inside it?

3. If the names of variables declared inside the procedure *conflict*—that is, are the same as names of variables declared outside the procedure—which declarations take precedence?

To examine the first two of these questions, consider Program SWAP1, which orders two integers X and Y according to their relative magnitudes and reports whether their original order has been swapped.

In Program SWAP1, the statements READ (X,Y) and WRITE (X,Y,C) direct the computer to read or write alphanumeric values from the keyboard and

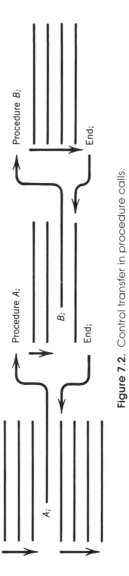

Figure 7.2. Control transfer in procedure calls.

PROGRAM SWAP1

```
program swap1 (input,output);
(* orders two numbers by nondecreasing value, and
   reports if they were swapped *)

var     x,y : real;
        c   : boolean;


  procedure reverse;
  (* swaps the values of x and y *)

  var  b : real;

  begin
    b := x;
    x := y;
    y := b
  end;    (* of reverse procedure *)


begin    (* main program *)
  read (x,y);

  if x > y
    then  begin
            reverse;
            c := true
          end
    else c := false;

  write (x, y, c)
end.   (* of swap1 program *)
```

type them on the screen. We will study this kind of statement in greater detail in Chapter 16. Note that this program does no graphics, therefore it does not include the graphic drivers.

Program SWAP1 includes a procedure called REVERSE, which uses the variables X and Y that were declared outside it. In addition, it uses another variable called B, which has been declared inside its body. Even though X and Y were not declared inside REVERSE, they are still usable in it, and their values are affected by the statements inside REVERSE. We call such variables *globals* since their scope includes the main body of the program as well as Procedure REVERSE. Variable B, on the other hand, is called a *local* variable since its scope includes only the body of Procedure REVERSE itself. It does not even exist outside the procedure. If we attempted to use it in the main program, the compiler would report an error regarding an "unknown identifier." Local variables lose their value along with their "life" as soon as their scope ends. Therefore, when we call the procedure again, local variables must be reinitialized; we may not assume that they retain their values from the last invocation.

Let us now consider Program SWAP2. It is identical to SWAP1 except that the local variable in Procedure REVERSE has been renamed "C," which happens also to be the name of a global variable.

In Program SWAP2 we have what seems to be a name conflict—two different variables (of different types, even) that bear the same name! To resolve such conflicts Pascal uses the rule that *local* identifiers supersede global ones if their

PROGRAM SWAP2

```
program swap2 (input,output);
(* orders two numbers by nondecreasing value, and
   reports if they were swapped *)

var   x,y : real;
      c    : boolean;


   procedure reverse;
   (* swaps the values of x and y *)

   var   c : real;

   begin
     c := x;
     x := y;
     y := c
   end; (* of reverse procedure *)


begin (* main program *)
  read (x,y);

  if x > y
    then   begin
             reverse;
             c := true
           end
      else c := false;

  write (x, y, c)
end.  (* of swap2 program *)
```

names are identical. This rule reinforces the concept of abstraction: Procedures, as semiautonomous entities within a program, should not be concerned with names of variables that were used outside their scope. Rather, they "block out" whatever they are not interested in, making their own declarations prevail. Outside of Procedure REVERSE, of course, it is the BOOLEAN variable C that prevails, rather than the variable C of type INTEGER that was declared inside the procedure.

We call the rules that govern the precedence of declarations *scope rules*. In summary, these rules state that:

1. Declared entities exist only within the environment of their declaration.
2. If several nested environments use the same identifier name, it is the declaration closest to the point where the name is used that prevails.

To see how these rules work, consider the following program framework that contains declarations, but no statements:

```
program a;

   var a,b : integer;
        c    : char;

   procedure p;

     var a,d : real;
          c    : integer;

   begin (* body of p *)
      (* point 1 *)

   end; (* of p procedure *)
begin (* body of a *)
   (* point 2 *)

end.  (* of a program *)
```

Which variables are visible at points 1 and 2 in the program, and what are their types? By applying the scope rules at point 1, we can readily identify A, D, and C as local variables with the data types that were associated with them inside Procedure P:

A,D of type REAL

C of type INTEGER

In addition to A,D and C, the global variable B declared in the main program, which is of type INTEGER, is also visible at point 1. However, the global variables A (of type INTEGER) and C (of type CHAR) are not visible at point 1 because the local variables A and C in Procedure P take precedence. So at point 1 we can "see" the following variables:

A,D of type REAL

B,C of type INTEGER

At point 2 only the global variables A, B, and C that were declared in the main program are "visible." The local variables that were declared inside the body of Procedure P no longer exist. Thus at point 2 we have

A,B of type INTEGER

C of type CHAR

The concepts of globality and locality apply also to the procedures themselves; for a procedure, like a variable, has to be declared in order to exist. Thus a procedure can be called only in the environment in which it was declared.

The ability to nest procedures within other procedures makes the concepts of locality and globality relative. If Procedure Q is nested within Procedure P, then any variable defined locally in P will be considered global in Q.

Communicating with Procedures

If a global variable is visible within a procedure—that is, there is no local variable by the same name to take precedence over it—then the value of that variable is passed into the procedure along with its name. This method of passing a value is called *inheritance*.

How can the values computed by the procedure be communicated back to its calling environment? One way is through the same global variables that carry the data into the procedure. Since the globals defined in the nesting environment are available for use inside the procedure body, they are affected by assignments to them, and thus can carry data—the results of computations performed inside the procedure—out to the calling environment. This communication method, however, is not very safe. It may happen that a procedure assigns values to global variables inadvertently, thereby overwriting the global values they formerly carried. When this happens, it is called a *side effect* of the procedure execution. A side effect cannot be anticipated by looking only at the statement that invokes the procedure, or by looking at the procedure in isolation. Rather, one must look at the procedure together with its environment, a task that is not always easy to do and that clearly contradicts the principle of abstraction.

The principle use of global variables in procedures is to enable these procedures to manipulate the global data structures used in the program. Since local variables cannot retain their value from one invocation of the procedure to the next, any values that are to exist for a longer duration must be assigned to global variables. Also, any values that are needed in other procedures or program segments can be communicated to those segments by being assigned to global variables.

The prevailing danger is that we may inadvertently change the value of a global variable that should not have been changed. Because of this danger, it is undesirable, though possible, to communicate with procedures by means of global variables. A better way to communicate data to a procedure is by means of *parameters.*

As seen in Program RECTANGLES2, parameters act as the gateway between the procedure and its environment. The procedure header contains a list of *parameters;* each invocation of the procedure includes a list of *arguments.* Each argument corresponds to one parameter. The parameters may be used in the body of the procedure just like any other local variables. They are not declared in the VAR declaration block within the procedure since their existence and their types are already known.

Depending on the application, we may choose one of two ways in which the arguments are related to the parameters. In some cases we may want the procedure to *know* the value of some variable in the environment and use that value to perform its task; but we do not want the procedure to *alter* the value of the variable. In other cases, we may want the procedure both to know and to alter the value.

The handling of parameters may be compared to the handling of information in a design office. Suppose that the architect wants the interior designer to work on a particular space. The interior designer will need to know the location of the walls and columns. The architect sends the designer a structural drawing that contains this information; the interior designer may *use* this information, but he cannot *change* the location of the walls or columns.

Now suppose that the architect reviews the structural drawing and finds that certain space requirements are not met. He may make some notes on the drawing and send it to the structural engineer. The engineer will both *use* and *change* the information on the drawing.

In Pascal, a parameter that the procedure can use but not change is called a *value parameter* or *simple parameter.* A parameter that the procedure can both use and change is called a *variable parameter* or *VAR parameter.*

Value parameters are used in Procedure DRAWRECTANGLE, which appears in Program RECTANGLES2, above. The main program determines the location for each rectangle and assigns the coordinates of the location to the arguments X and Y. When DRAWRECTANGLE is called, the values of arguments X and Y are assigned to the corresponding parameters, R and S. DRAWRECTANGLE uses the values of R and S to draw the rectangle. As it happens,

DRAWRECTANGLE does not change the values of R and S—but even if it did, this would not affect the value of the arguments X and Y. The parameter R has its own memory cell, independent of the argument X; likewise, S is independent of Y. No matter what happens to R and S, the values of X and Y are unchanged. DRAWRECTANGLE is like the interior designer: To guarantee that the structural plan is not inadvertently altered, we send him a *copy* of the drawing and not the original.

Variable parameters are used in Procedure REVERSE, in Program SWAP3, as indicated by the keyword VAR in the procedure header. Here it is essential for the procedure not only to know the values of X and Y, but also to assign them new values—namely, to assign the value of X to Y and the value of Y to X. We

PROGRAM SWAP3

```
program swap3 (input,output);
(* orders two numbers by nondecreasing value, and
   reports if they were swapped *)

var   x,y : real;
       c  : boolean;


   procedure reverse (var p,q : real);
   (* swaps the values of x and y *)

   var  b : real;

   begin
     b := p;
     p := q;
     q := b
   end; (* of reverse procedure *)


begin (* main program *)
  read (x,y);

  if x > y
    then  begin
            reverse(x,y);
            c := true
          end
    else c := false;

  write (x, y, c)
end.   (* of swap3 program *)
```

accomplish this by sending Procedure REVERSE the *memory address* of X and Y instead of their *values*. The parameter P becomes *another identifier* for the memory cell that is also identified by X; likewise Q becomes another identifier for Y. Whatever happens to P and Q also happens *automatically* to X and Y. Thus REVERSE is like the structural engineer who works on the *original* structural drawing, not just a copy of it.

The rules for using value parameters (simple parameters) and variable parameters (VAR parameters) are as follows:

1. Both value parameters and variable parameters must be declared in the procedure header. The argument list must be provided each time the procedure is invoked, and must correspond in number and type to the parameters.

2. The keyword VAR in the parameter list indicates that the parameters following it (up to the nearest semicolon) are VAR parameters; any parameters not preceded by VAR are value parameters.

3. Value parameters and VAR parameters may be mixed in the same procedure header.

4. An argument that is passed through a value parameter may be a variable, a constant, a literal, or an expression, as long as its value is of the same type as the corresponding parameter. An argument that is passed through a VAR parameter must be a *variable* of the same type as the parameter.

5. The procedure may operate on both value parameters and VAR parameters, just like any other variable within its scope. However, any changes in a value parameter remain isolated from the argument and are not returned to the calling environment, whereas changes in a VAR parameter are automatically communicated to the calling environment.

□ FUNCTIONS

Procedures make it possible to abstract sets of operations—that is, encapsulate them into a module that we can refer to by a name. Pascal provides another abstraction mechanism that makes it possible to encapsulate expressions. These encapsulated expressions can be used just like any other expression: They can be used as operands in other expressions, and they can be assigned to variables. The programming construct that enables us to perform such abstractions is called a *function*. We have already seen a few standard functions that are provided by Pascal: ABS, TRUNC, ROUND, SQR, SQRT, and so on. We shall now learn how to create our own functions to encapsulate expressions that are more complex than those provided by the language.

The structure of a function is very similar to that of a procedure, but since it may be assigned to a variable, it must yield a single value of a specific type. For example, we may want to use a function such as

```
y := max (p,q);
```

that assigns to a variable called Y the larger of the two numbers P and Q. This is obviously an abstraction of the following structure:

```
if p > q
   then y := p
   else y := q;
```

but it is much shorter and intuitively easier to understand. This example is embedded in Program MAXNUM.

In Program MAXNUM, MAX is the name of the function; P and Q are its parameters, which are of type INTEGER. The type of the value that is calculated by function MAX is also of type INTEGER. This fact is expressed by adding a type declaration after the parameter list:

```
function max (p,q : integer) : integer;
```

PROGRAM MAXNUM

```
program maxnum (input,output);
(* writes out the larger of two input value *)

var   x,y,z : integer;


  function max (p,q : integer) : integer;
  (* returns the value of p or q, whichever is
     greater *)

  begin
    if p > q
      then  max := p
      else  max := q
  end;  (* of max function *)


begin (* main body of maxnum *)
  read(x,y);
  z := max(x,y);
  write(z)
end.  (* of maxnum program *)
```

A function, like a procedure, may have simple and VAR parameters in its parameter list, and its body may include any statements. But unlike a procedure, a function must include a statement that explicitly assigns some value to the identifying name of the function. The assignment statement may occur in a single line, usually at the end of the function, or in more than one line, as in the Program MAXNUM. The name of the function may not be used as an intermediary variable inside the body. The assignment statement defines the value returned by the function. Without such an assignment, that value would be undefined.

If the function is to calculate more than one result, it should be defined as a procedure rather than as a function since side effects are very undesirable in functions.

☐ RECURSION

When we began our discussion of procedures and functions, we mentioned that they may call other procedures and functions. A question that arises immediately is, then, can procedures and functions call themselves?

The answer is yes. Furthermore, this process is one of the most powerful features of high-level programming languages. It even has a name of its own: *recursion*. Recursion, when properly used, allows us to solve a problem by means of simpler versions of the same problem. By doing so we greatly improve the clarity of the solution, and we reduce considerably the amount of code that actually needs to be written.

An object is said to be recursive if it consists of, or is defined in terms of itself. Maurits C. Escher's famous Print Gallery lithograph (1956) is a visual expression of recursion, where the viewer is presented with pictures in a gallery, one of which is a picture of the gallery itself, including the picture depicting the gallery. . . .

The appeal of recursion to mathematicians, artists, composers (like J. S. Bach), and to programmers lies in its ability to capture an infinite series of objects or compositions within a finite statement, without repetition.

The mechanism that makes recursion possible in programming is that of scope rules. As we mentioned earlier, the variables that are local to a procedure are created dynamically upon entering that procedure and destroyed upon exiting it. In the case of recursion, the original procedure is still active when it calls itself. Since we have not yet exited from the original procedure, the variables that were created when it was invoked still exist. When the procedure calls itself, new variables are created, but the original variables remain intact. In other words, a recursive procedure creates and invokes another procedure identical to itself. Thus while reducing the amount of code that needs to be written by the programmer, recursion does not really save any computing time.

To demonstrate recursion, let us start with a very simple problem of computing the sum of all integers from 1 up to some number N:

$$SUM = 1 + 2 + 3 + \cdots + N$$

We could express this as

$$SUM = (1 + 2 + 3 + \cdots + N - 1) + N$$

meaning that we compute the sum by adding the last integer, N, to the sum of all the integers from 1 up to $N-1$, while noting that the solution is trivial if $N = 1$. This process is demonstrated by Program SUMUP.

Tracing the execution of this program for NUMBER = 3, we see that at first SUM is invoked with the parameter $M = 3$. Since $M <> 1$, another invocation

PROGRAM SUMUP

```
program sumup (input,output);
(* computes the sum of integers 1 through user-
   defined number, recursively *)

var    number,total : integer;

   function sum (m : integer) : integer;
   (* computes the sum of integers 1 though m,
      recursively *)

   begin
     if m = 1
       then  sum := 1
       else  sum := sum (m - 1) + m
   end; (* of sum function *)

begin  (* main program *)
   read (number);
   total := sum (number);
   write (total)
end.  (* of sumup program *)
```

of SUM occurs, this time with $M = 2$. Again $M < > 1$, therefore a third invocation occurs, with $M = 1$, so we assign

SUM := 1

This completes the third invocation and returns control to the uncompleted second invocation, where SUM is assigned

SUM := SUM (1) + 2

that results in

SUM = 3

This completes the second invocation and returns control to the uncompleted first invocation. There we assign

SUM := SUM (2) + 3

that results in

SUM = 6

and this completes the first invocation.

You may have noticed that this is not the most efficient way to compute this sum since

SUM = $N*(N + 1)/2$

but it demonstrates in a simple way the principle of recursion.

A more interesting use of recursion is demonstrated by Program SIERPINSKICURVE, whose well-known output is shown in Figure 7.3.

In general, every recursive procedure could also be written as an iteration, but care must be taken not to destroy intermediate results. In the example of Program SIERPINSKICURVE, the iterative version would require the use of many more variables to store intermediate endpoints of each new line segment. The recursive version supplies the additional variables and the desired protection implicitly through the recursion mechanism.

PROGRAM SIERPINSKICURVE

```
program sierpinskicurve (output);
(* draws the sierpinski curve, recursively *)

#include "drivers.i"

const   level     = 1;
        screensize = 512;

var     i, h, x, y, x0, y0 : integer;

  procedure a (i : integer); forward;
  procedure b (i : integer); forward;
  procedure c (i : integer); forward;
  procedure d (i : integer); forward;


  procedure a;

  begin
    if i > 0
      then begin
              a (i-1);  x := x + h;  y := y - h;
              drawto (x,y);
              b (i-1);  x := x + 2*h;
              drawto (x,y);
              d (i-1);  x := x + h;  y := y + h;
              drawto (x,y);
              a (i-1)
           end
  end;  (* a procedure *)


  procedure b;

  begin
    if i > 0
      then begin
              b (i-1);  x := x - h;  y := y - h;
              drawto (x,y);
              c (i-1);                y := y - 2*h;
              drawto (x,y);
              a (i-1);  x := x + h;  y := y - h;
              drawto (x,y);
              b (i-1)
           end
  end;  (* b procedure *)
```

```
procedure c;

begin
  if i > 0
    then begin
            c (i-1);  x := x - h;   y := y + h;
            drawto (x,y);
            d (i-1);  x := x - 2*h;
            drawto (x,y);
            b (i-1);  x := x - h;   y := y - h;
            drawto (x,y);
            c (i-1)
         end
end;  (* c procedure *)


procedure d;

begin
  if i > 0
    then begin
            d (i-1);  x := x + h;   y := y + h;
            drawto (x,y);
            a (i-1);  y := y + 2*h;
            drawto (x,y);
            c (i-1);  x := x - h;   y := y + h;
            drawto (x,y);
            d (i-1)
         end
end;  (* d procedure *)


begin (* main program *)
  entergraphicsmode;

  h := screensize div 4;   x0 := 2*h;   y0 := 3*h;

  for  i := 1 to level do
    begin
      x0 := x0 - h;   h := h div 2;   y0 := y0 + h;
      x  := x0;                       y  := y0;
      moveto (x,y);

      a (i);  x := x + h;  y := y - h;
      drawto (x,y);
      b (i);  x := x - h;  y := y - h;
      drawto (x,y);
      c (i);  x := x - h;  y := y + h;
```

```
   drawto (x,y);
   d (i);   x := x + h;   y := y + h;
   drawto (x,y)
 end;

leavegraphicsmode
end.   (* of sierpinski curve program *)
```

□ FORWARD REFERENCING AND EXTERNALS

One restriction Pascal imposes on programmers is that every variable, procedure, or function must be declared *before* it can be used. Thus a procedure (or
function) may not be called from another procedure at the same or higher level
of nesting, unless the procedure being called appears first in the text of the program. If two procedures are mutually recursive—that is, if each one calls the

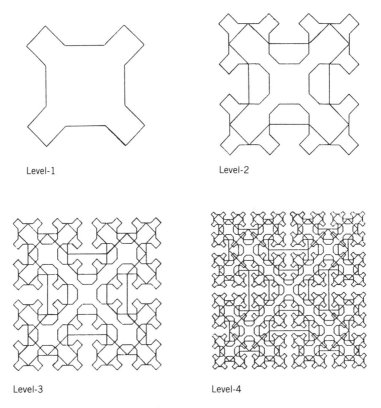

Level-1   Level-2

Level-3   Level-4

Figure 7.3. The Sierpinski curve.

other, as is the case in Program SIERPINSKICURVE—it is impossible for them both to appear before their calls. Consider the following stylized example.

```
procedure a;
  begin
    (* call procedure b *)
  end;

procedure b;
  begin
    (* call procedure a *)
  end;
```

To make such a construct possible, Pascal provides a mechanism called *forward referencing*. With this mechanism a call to a procedure (or function) may precede the full definition of that procedure, provided that the program is aware at that point that the procedure exists and that it will be fully detailed at some later place. To create a forward reference, the header of the procedure is separated from its body and placed in the program before the procedure is ever called; the reserved word FORWARD is appended to the header. FORWARD thus replaces the body of the procedure at the point of its declaration. The body of the procedure may appear much later in the program, possibly after the declaration of some other procedures. The full header of the procedure is *not* repeated, and the actual body is identified by the name alone.

This separation of the body from the header allows the procedure to be called from other procedures that are declared between the header and the body. It also allows the procedure to call such other procedures, thereby resolving the problem of mutually recursive constructs, as it was demonstrated by Program SIERPINSKICURVE. A similar mechanism permits Pascal programs, in most compilers, to call procedures that are not part of the program text itself—that is, they are written in a separate procedure library. Such libraries of procedures are written by experts for particular applications, and are usually sophisticated and comprehensive. They relieve the programmer from having to solve problems for which the solutions are already well known. One such library of routines contains all of the graphic utilities we have seen so far—ENTERGRAPHICSMODE, DRAWTO, and so on. These routines appear in Appendix B.

External procedures and functions are declared by replacing their body with the word EXTERNAL. They must be loaded explicitly along with the compiled program (after they themselves have been compiled), so that when the execution of the program reaches the point where they are called, it will be able to execute the instructions that are contained in the external routines.

Program MENU3 demonstrates all that we have learned in this chapter about the use of procedures and functions. Essentially, it is a more readable rewrite of Program MENU2 from Chapter 6. This clarity is achieved by moving the circle-drawing part from the main control structure into a procedure called CIRCLE,

PROGRAM MENU3

```pascal
program menu3 (input,output);
(* draws multiple disconnected lines and circles,
   selectable interactively by the user *)

# include "drivers.i"

var   x,y, mode : integer;


  procedure circle (cx,cy : integer);
  (* determines radius through user-input, then
     draws circle centered at <cx,cy> *)

  const   radians        = 0.0174533;
          approx         = 72;

  var     radius, x,y,i : integer;
          theta,r,dx,dy : real;
  begin
    (* get second point *)
    readcursorlocation (x,y);

    (* compute radius  *)
    r := sqrt(sqr(cx - x) + sqr(cy - y));
    radius := round(r);

    (* draw circle *)
    moveto ((cx + radius), cy);

    for i := 1 to approx do
      begin
        theta := (i*360/approx)*radians;

        dx := radius*cos(theta);
        dy := radius*sin(theta);

        x := cx + round(dx);
        y := cy + round(dy);

        drawto (x,y)
      end
  end; (* of circle procedure *)


  function command (x,y : integer) : integer;
  (* determines which mode has been selected by
     the user *)
```

```
   begin
     if x < 350
       then  command := 2              (* "newline" *)
       else  if x < 700
               then  command := 1    (* "circle"  *)
               else  command := 4    (* "quit"    *)
   end; (* of command function *)


   procedure drawmenuboxes;
   (* draws menu boxes *)

   begin
     moveto (   0, 70);    drawto (1000, 70);
     moveto ( 350, 70);    drawto ( 350,  0);
     moveto ( 700, 70);    drawto ( 700,  0)
   end;  (* of drawmenuboxes procedure *)


begin (* menu3 program *)
   entergraphicsmode;
   drawmenuboxes;
   mode := 2;   (* moveto *)

   repeat
     readcursorlocation (x,y);    (* get command *)
     if y < 70
       then  mode := command (x,y)
       else case mode of      (* execute command *)
              1: begin
                   circle (x,y);
                   mode := 2            (* newline *)
                 end;

              2: begin
                   moveto (x,y);
                   mode := 3;          (* drawline *)
                 end;

              3: drawto (x,y);

              4: ;
            end;   (* case of mode *)
   until (mode = 4);

   leavegraphicsmode
end.  (* of menu3 program *)
```

by putting the part that parses the commands into a function called COM-MAND (which returns an integer value representing the selected mode), and by putting the menu box drawing utilities in a separate procedure called DRAW-MENUBOXES. Note how some global variables and constants have been made local to the circle-drawing routine, thereby further enhancing the readability of the program.

□ SUMMARY

As we add features to a program, it becomes more complex. To manage the complexity, we need to employ the principles of *abstraction* and *partitioning,* by which we group the variables and statements that pertain to an operation into a single package, known as a PROCEDURE or a FUNCTION, which we can call by name.

A procedure declaration, like a program, consists of CONST and VAR declarations and a body, which contains one or more statements. In addition, the header of a procedure may contain a list of *parameters,* which are variables that act as the gateway between the procedure and its calling environment.

To *invoke* a procedure in the body of the program we simply write its name, followed by its parameters, if any, in parentheses.

The *scope rules* provide that *local* variables—those that are declared within a procedure—exist only within the procedure, and only for as long as the procedure is executing. Variables that are *global* to the procedure—that is, they belong to the calling environment—can be used and altered within the procedure, provided that there is no local variable with the same name as the global variable. If there is, then the local variable takes precedence, and the global variable is "invisible" to the procedure.

When global variables are used within a procedure, undesired side effects may occur. It is preferable to communicate with the procedure by means of explicit *parameters. Value parameters* carry a value from the calling environment to the procedure; any changes that occur within the procedure are *not* carried back to the environment. If we wish these changes to be carried back, then we use *VAR parameters* instead.

Procedures may be nested within other procedures and may call other procedures. A procedure may even call itself, in a process known as *recursion.* We can invoke a procedure outside the program by means of an EXTERNAL declaration, and we can invoke a procedure before its full declaration appears in the program by means of a FORWARD declaration.

A FUNCTION is structured much like a procedure, except that it must be evaluated to a specific type. The type is declared in the function header, and the evaluation is assigned within the body of the function.

8

EXERCISE 2

Using the looping and control constructs discussed in this part of the book, and the abstraction and partitioning principles, write an interactive, menu-driven graphic program that lets the user choose between LINE, CIRCLE, TRIANGLE, and RECTANGLE drawing utilities. All these figures should be stored *procedurally,* that is—defined in your program as parameterized procedures. The parameters that you provide should let the user position and scale the figures interactively, anywhere in the drawing area.

The user should be able to pick the desired figures from a menu. Since we have not yet discussed how to label menu boxes textually, and also because it makes more sense from a graphic design point of view, the menu boxes should be labeled *iconically,* by small graphical symbols that represent the option each menu box stands for. For example, if a certain menu box provides the option to draw a circle—the "label" in that box should be a small circle. Figure 8.1 shows an example of such an iconic menu.

The icons in the menu boxes should be drawn by the *same* procedures that are used *by the user* to draw the figures. In other words, your program should contain only *one* set of figure-drawing procedures that are used both interactively—by the user—and noninteractively—by the menu-drawing part of the program itself.

This can be achieved if the procedure for drawing each figure does *not* communicate with the user directly, but instead takes its arguments from another procedure that performs such user interaction, or from constants within the program itself. For example, the CIRCLE drawing procedure in Program MENU3 *does* interact with the user through the command READCURSORLOCATION, which is embedded in it. It could not, therefore, be used to draw the icon of a circle in the appropriate menu box. If, however, it were modified to accept RADIUS as a parameter, rather than compute it from user input, then it could be used for both purposes (i.e., user interaction and icon drawing). The position of the circle and its radius could then be supplied by another procedure, such as

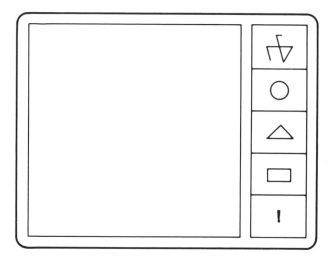

Figure 8.1. An iconic menu.

PROGRAM PUTCIRCLE

```
procedure putcircle;
(* reads  two cursor locations and determines the
   location of the circle and its radius. it than
   calls   procedure   circle   with   the   computed
   parameters to draw the circle itself. *)

var     x1,y1, x2,y2, radius, dx,dy : integer;

begin
  readcursorlocation (x1,y1);
  readcursorlocation (x2,y2);

  dx := x1 - x2;
  dy := y1 - y2;
  radius := round(sqrt(sqr(dx) + sqr(dy)));

  circle (x1,y1, radius)
end;   (* of putcircle procedure *)
```

PUTCIRCLE, which will get two input points from the user. Then it will compute the radius, and finally call Procedure CIRCLE itself using the computed arguments. Alternatively, Procedure CIRCLE could be called directly from within Procedure DRAWMENUBOXES, in which case its position and radius will be given through constants since the location of the icon and its size can easily be predetermined by the programmer.

The advantages of using only one set of figure-drawing procedures for both user interactive positioning/scaling of figures, and for drawing the icons in the menu boxes, are threefold:

1. The icons in the menu boxes represent *exactly* what they stand for.
2. The code is more compact (one procedure for each figure instead of two), and more reliable: It needs to be debugged only once.
3. Changes are easy to make: If you decide to replace the CIRCLE drawing utility with, say, a HEXAGON drawing utility, only one procedure needs to be modified.

PART THREE

DATA STRUCTURES

9
SCALARS

So far we have discussed several means for drawing lines on the screen of a graphic terminal, along with some means to control and direct this operation. We have, however, assumed that the user never makes any mistakes; at least we provided no means to correct them, such as erasing erroneous lines. Obviously, this assumption of perfection is unrealistic. By its very nature, design is an iterative process of purposeful trial and error, and many changes to the drawing will be needed before it is complete.

How, then, can we provide the user with the important feature of changing what he has already drawn? One simple solution to the problem is to provide the user with means to mark erroneous lines, then direct the computer to redraw the entire picture, except for the figure (or figures) that were marked for deletion. Another way would be to "undraw" the marked figure, by drawing on top of it in the background color (typically in black). For the sake of keeping the graphic display drivers simple, in this book we shall proceed with the first technique, although both techniques are equally suitable.

In order for the computer to perform such a feat, two amenities must be provided:

1. A way for the computer to *store* the picture in its memory as the user draws it, so that it will be able to redraw it when so directed.
2. A way of indicating to the system that a line is to be removed from the stored picture, so that when the picture is redrawn, that line will not reappear.

It is the first of these two amenities that is more difficult to achieve. It introduces the concept of storing data that does not yet exist at the time the program is being written, but rather is generated by the user as a function of executing the program after it is compiled. The programmer must therefore anticipate the nature and quantity of the data that will be produced by the user, and provide some means to store it. In other words, the programmer must build into the program the means to store data in some retrievable way.

Once the data has been stored, it is a relatively simple matter to search it for the item the user wishes to delete, and remove that item from storage. The remaining items can be redrawn, after the screen has been cleared.

In this part of the book we will study the important component of programming called the *structuring of the data*. This component, together with the operations we studied earlier, comprises the mathematical symbolic representation of real-world environments and artifacts and provides the basis for graphic display and analysis. We will deal here only with the fundamental concepts of data structuring; more detailed study of these concepts as they pertain to modeling physical artifacts is described in great detail in the second volume of this series.

☐ DATA STRUCTURES

We have already seen what data types are, in principle, and have discussed some of their uses. More generally, the concept of a data type originated from broad mathematical and logical reasoning, and is used in programming languages to remove ambiguities and to explicitly identify the range of permissible values and operations. Data types are also part of the abstraction principles that we discussed earlier in terms of procedures and functions. Just as procedures and functions enable the programmer to encapsulate a group of operations or an expression into one named unit, data types enable encapsulation of the data used by such operations into meaningful structures.

Data types thus fulfill two important purposes:

1. They allow us to structure a program in terms of the problem it addresses rather than in terms of the specific programming language in which it is written. For example, in our graphic applications it will allow us to use such terms as points, lines, figures, and drawings rather than integers and reals. Consequently, programs become easier to write, easier to read, and easier to debug and maintain.

2. Data types convey to the compiler more information about the range and the associations of the values that a program uses, thereby enabling it to optimize the object code and perform more extensive error checking. Consequently, programs become easier to debug, and they run faster.

Pascal makes it possible to exploit the concept of data typing almost to the full extent defined by its mathematical basis. The rules governing data typing in Pascal are:

1. Every item, whether it is a constant, a variable, a function, or an expression, is of one and only one type. This type does not change in the course of

the program. The type of the item determines a *domain*—that is, a set of possible values, only one of which may be assumed by that item at any time.

2. A limited set of operators is defined for each type. This limitation guarantees that only legal values will be assigned to variables of a given type. The programmer may extend this set of operators by defining his own procedures and functions, in which case he must assume the responsibility for type compatibility.

3. The nature of a data type is syntactical; that is, the type of any item may always be deduced by examining the text of the program, without necessarily executing it. This enables the compiler to perform type checking, a beneficial result.

Most often the problems that we address do not dictate any unique choice of data representation, any more than they dictate the representation of operations. The choice of data representation is one of the major decisions that has to be made by the programmer in the course of composing a program; it has profound effects on the ease with which the steps of the program can be conceived, and on the efficiency of its execution. Therefore, time spent on designing a good data structure is time well spent, and should not be compromised. It is easier to replace a procedure (an operation) with a better one than to change the data structure after it has been used to write many pages of code.

Types in Pascal can be divided into two categories:

1. Simple types.
2. Compound types.

A variable of a simple type is made of a single, indivisible value, whereas a variable of a compound type is actually an ensemble of several values. In a graphics program we often find the individual values of X and Y, each of them a simple type (in this case, type INTEGER). A pair of X and Y values defines a point, which is a compound type composed of two coordinate values. Lines are another compound type, being made of two points, or four coordinate values. An entire drawing is an ensemble of lines, and a project is an ensemble of drawings.

In this chapter we will consider the simple types, and in the following ones we will consider the various kinds of compound types.

☐ SIMPLE TYPES

Simple types are also known as *scalar* types. A scalar is an indivisible unit of data that is treated as a single, complete entity. A scalar does not have subfields or components that can be manipulated independently. The most familiar scalars are the standard, elementary types: INTEGER, REAL, BOOLEAN, and CHAR. The programmer may, however, extend this limited selection by declaring his own scalar types. Such declared types fall into one of two categories:

1. Enumerated types.
2. Subrange types.

Enumerated Types

Enumerated types are the simplest of all the data types that are declarable by the programmer. They are defined simply by listing, or enumerating, their literals, which are assumed to represent distinct and unequal values. The only operators that are automatically defined for them are assignment and equality. Additional computational power is achieved by imposing on them a linear ordering, thus allowing the use of the relational operators <, < =, < >, = >, and > and the operators PRED (predecessor) and SUCC (successor).

Obviously, nonstandard data types must be declared if they are to be recognized by the computer. There are two methods of declaring an enumerated type. In the first method, we declare the type explicitly and give it a name. Then we can declare any number of variables of that type. In the second method, we associate a variable directly with the type definition. The type then has no name, and therefore cannot be used with other variables.

Using the first method we could, for example, declare an enumerated type called DAY:

```
type   day = (sun, mon, tue, wed, thu, fri, sat);
```

DAY is the name of a new type that includes seven different values, in the same sense that BOOLEAN is the name of a type that includes only two values (TRUE and FALSE). SUN, MON, TUE, WED, THU, WED, FRI, and SAT are the specific *values* that may be assigned to a variable of type DAY, just as TRUE and FALSE are the values that may be assigned to a variable of type BOOLEAN.

DAY can be used to define a variable (or many variables) of this new type; for example,

```
var   dayofweek : day;
```

The variable DAYOFWEEK can now be assigned any one of the seven values of type DAY; for example,

```
dayofweek := sun;
```

An identifier used as a value cannot also be used for some other purpose. Since SUN is a value in this example, we could not also have a variable with the same name.

Using the second method instead of the first, we can associate a variable directly with the enumeration of values:

```
var dayofweek : (sun, mon, tue, wed, thu, fri, sat);
```

This method is, however, not recommended because it is not as clear to the reader as the first method. Furthermore, although it can be used for declaring the variables on the left-hand side of the colon as members of this particular enumerated type, this method cannot be used to declare parameters of procedures or functions as members of that same type as the global variables.

The TYPE declaration, like the CONST and VAR declarations, appears at the beginning of the program, procedure, or function, between the CONST and the VAR declaration blocks.

The values that are used in an enumerated type declaration must be unique; that is, a single value may not belong to more than one enumerated type (within the same scope). Therefore, the following declaration is *illegal:*

```
type day     = (mon, tue, wed, thu, fri, sat, sun);
     weekend = (sat, sun);
```

because SAT and SUN are components (values) of two different data types.

As with type BOOLEAN, the values of an enumerated type are also its literals. Thus we can assign them directly to variables of the type. If we declare

```
type  buildingpart = (wall, window, door);
var   part : buildingpart;
```

we may then assign

```
part := wall
```

As with other types, mixed assignments are not permitted. The following are *illegal* assignments:

```
day := wall;
part := mon
```

As stated earlier, the only operators that are automatically defined for scalar type variables are the assignment and the relationals (that result in a boolean-valued expression). The relationals can be used for an enumerated type because there is an implicit order to its values, defined by the order in which they were enumerated in the type declaration. In type DAY, for example, we have

SUN < MON
MON < FRI
WED > TUE

However, if we declared

```
type  day = (sun, sat, fri, mon, tue, wed, thu);
```

instead of the original declaration, then we could have

SUN < MON
MON > FRI

Similarly, having declared

```
type  buildingpart = (wall, window, door);
```

we have

WALL < WINDOW
WINDOW < DOOR

Since enumerated types are ordered, we can apply the standard functions PRED and SUCC to them. They will return a value of the same type as the argument. For example,

PRED(WINDOW) yields WALL
SUCC(WINDOW) yields DOOR

Note that the first member of the type has no predecessor, and the last member has no successor!

Applying the function ORD to a value of an enumerated type returns an integer, which is the ordinal number of the value in its definition list. The first value in the list has the ordinal number zero. Thus

ORD(WALL) = 0
ORD(DOOR) = 2

Because they are ordered, we may also use the FOR loop directly on enumerated types. For example,

```
for part := wall to door do
   (* ... body of the loop ... *)
```

Similarly, enumerated types can (and often are) used as selectors in a CASE statement. This usage is implemented in Program MENU4, which is very similar to Program MENU3 that we saw earlier, except that the value returned by Function COMMAND is from the enumerated type ACTION, which includes DRAWCIRCLE, NEWLINE, DRAWLINE, and STOP.

To summarize, the properties of the enumerated type are:

1. The values are distinct from each other and from the values of any other type.
2. The values are ordered.
3. The assignment operation is defined.
4. All the relational operations are defined.
5. A variable of any enumerated type may be used as:
   5.1. The argument of the standard functions ORD, PRED, and SUCC.
   5.2. The selector in a CASE statement.
   5.3. The control variable in a FOR loop.

Subrange Types

The other scalar (simple) type in Pascal is the *subrange* type, which provides for many circumstances when a variable, declared to be of a certain scalar type, is known in advance to assume only a limited subset of all the possible values in the domain of that type. For example, the X and Y coordinates of the points and lines we draw on a graphic display terminal are of type INTEGER, but their values are limited to a small subset of all the integers. Typically, the range of meaningful values is from 0 through 1023 for X and smaller than that for Y. Knowing this property in advance, we can limit the range of integers that we tell the program to use, thereby saving memory space, optimizing the execution, and—most important—making the program more readable. A reader of the program, who is knowledgeable about computer graphics, upon seeing the range 0 through 1023 associated with the variables X and Y may deduce that X and Y are most likely used for representing the screen location of points, rather than for something else.

In Pascal, for every scalar type (except REAL) it is possible to create a new type whose values are a subrange of the values of the original type. The original type is then referred to as the *associated* scalar type. A subrange type retains all

PROGRAM MENU4

```pascal
program menu4 (input,output);
(* draws multiple disconnected lines and circles,
   selectable interactively  by the user *)

# include "drivers.i"

type  action = (drawcircle, newline, drawline,
                stop);

var   x,y    : integer;
      quit   : boolean;
      mode   : action;


  procedure circle (cx,cy : integer);
  (* determines radius through user-input, then
     draws circle centered at <cx,cy> *)

  const  radians       = 0.0174533;
         approx        = 72;

  var    radius, x,y,i : integer;
         theta,r,dx,dy : real;
  begin
    (* get second point *)
    readcursorlocation (x,y);

    (* compute radius  *)
    r := sqrt(sqr(cx - x) + sqr(cy - y));
    radius := round(r);

    (* draw circle *)
    moveto ((cx + radius), cy);

    for i := 1 to approx do
      begin
        theta := (i*360/approx)*radians;

        dx := radius*cos(theta);
        dy := radius*sin(theta);

        x := cx + round(dx);
        y := cy + round(dy);

        drawto (x,y)
      end
  end; (* of circle procedure *)
```

```
function command (x,y : integer) : action;
(* determines which mode has been selected by
   the user *)

begin
  if x < 350
    then  command := newline
    else  if x < 700
            then  command := drawcircle
            else  command := stop
end; (* of command function *)


procedure drawmenuboxes;
(* draws menu boxes *)

begin
  moveto (   0, 70);    drawto (1000, 70);
  moveto ( 350, 70);    drawto ( 350,  0);
  moveto ( 700, 70);    drawto ( 700,  0)
end;  (* of drawmenuboxes procedure *)


begin (* menu4 program *)
  entergraphicsmode;

  drawmenuboxes;

  quit := false;                (* initialization *)
  mode := newline;

  repeat
    readcursorlocation (x,y);    (* get command *)

    if y < 70
      then mode := command(x,y)
      else case mode of        (* execute command *)
             drawcircle : begin
                            circle (x,y);
                            mode := newline
                          end;

             newline    : begin
                            moveto (x,y);
                            mode := drawline
                          end;

             drawline   : drawto (x,y);
```

```
          stop          : quit := true
       end (* case of mode *)
  until quit;

  leavegraphicsmode
end.  (* of menu4 program *)
```

the properties of the associated type, with an additional restriction on the range of its values. This range is defined by two constants that are members of the associated type. For example, in

```
type   index = 1..20;
```

the associated type is INTEGER, and in

```
type   letter = 'a'..'z';
```

the associated type is CHAR. Similarly, for the associated enumerated type,

```
type   day = (mon, tue, wed, thu, fri, sat, sun);
```

we may define subrange types such as

```
weekday = mon..fri;
weekend = sat..sun
```

The constants that are used in the subrange definition are called its *lower bound* and *upper bound*. The declaration is acceptable only if the lower bound is less than or equal to the upper bound, and there is at least one element in the range.

All the functions and operations defined for the associated scalar type may be used with the subrange type. However, we may not assign a value to a subrange type variable beyond its range. It is the programmer's responsibility to ensure that no out-of-range assignment can occur, for the compiler cannot determine what value may be assigned to the variable of the subrange type in the course of executing the program. If an out-of-range assignment does occur, it will cause a run-time error.

☐ SUMMARY

To enable the user to change what he has already drawn on the screen, the computer must be able to *store* the picture. The key to storage is creating a *data structure,* which organizes data into meaningful units and permits the compiler to perform extensive error checking.

Pascal requires that every constant, variable, function, and expression be of a defined type. For each type a limited set of operators is defined, so that only legal values may be assigned to variables of that type.

A *simple* or *scalar* type variable is made of a single value. A *compound* type variable is an ensemble of several values.

Pascal provides four standard scalar types: INTEGER, REAL, BOOLEAN, and CHAR. The programmer may define additional types, which may be *enumerated* or *subrange* types.

An *enumerated* type can be declared explicitly by stating the name of the type and listing, or enumerating, all its possible values. Variables may then be declared to be of that type. Alternatively, an enumerated type can be declared by associating a variable directly with the list of values. The values of an enumerated type may not be used by any other type (within the same scope).

Variables of an enumerated type are ordered, as defined by the order in which they are enumerated in the declaration. The assignment operator and the relational operators may be applied to variables of an enumerated type.

A *subrange* type is always *associated* with another type. The domain of the subrange type is a subset of the domain of the associated type. The subrange type is defined by listing two constants, the *lower bound* and the *upper bound,* which are members of the associated type. A subrange type variable has all the properties of the associated type, except that no value may be assigned to it that exceeds the bounds.

10

ARRAYS

In Chapter 9 we discussed scalar types in which each value is an indivisible unit. While indivisible values often meet our needs, there are also many occasions when we must deal with collections of related values. In fact, it is frequently the case that the relations between the values are at least as important as the values themselves. Consider, for example, two of the many different ways four points can be connected by lines, depicted in Figure 10.1

To learn how to deal with such cases, we now turn our discussion to types whose purpose is keeping collections of things organized. Such collections are called *data structures;* the things being collected are called the *elements* of the structure; and a type whose values are data structures is called a nonscalar or a *structured* type.

As the name implies, structured data types are formed by collecting simpler components into a composite structure. Consequently, a structured data type is defined in terms of one or more previously defined data types, called the constituent or *base* types. The base types are collected into a composite by means of well-defined structuring methods. A value of a structured type thus consists of components that are values of its constituent types.

A good metaphor is a family unit, which we may define as a single entity that is made of individual members. For some applications, such as counting the number of children, we may need to know what is the age of each family member. For other applications, such as calculating the gross average income of a certain population, we may not be concerned with the individual members, but with the family as a whole.

Like all other data types, structured types have a domain of values and a set of operations that are defined on these values. There are, however, two kinds of operations that are unique to structured types. These are the *construction* and *selection* operations that allow us to access the individual components of a structure—like the individual members in the family metaphor. Construction operators allow us to add and remove elements of a given structure, while selection

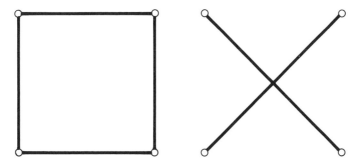

Figure 10.1. Different associations of the same four points.

operators allow us to update or otherwise use the value of such components—as in computing the number of children in the family.

The most common usage of structured data types is for collection and storage of information generated while the program is running. In graphic applications, we can store all the lines drawn by a user on the screen and reproduce them upon request. This method builds an internal representation of what the user does, which we call a *model*. Using the model, we can correct errors and otherwise modify a drawing. The user can delete the erroneous sections from the stored representation, then erase the screen and redraw it with the stored data. Since the erroneous parts are no longer stored, they will not be redrawn; the effect will be the same as erasing them from the screen.

Pascal offers us several different structured types that can be utilized for the purposes of storing data. As in the case of looping constructs studied in Chapter 5, there are usually several structures that can be utilized for a given task. We must select the one most suitable for the task at hand, so the program will be as efficient as possible.

In this chapter we will study one of the simplest structured data type, the *array*, which stores individual values in an *indexed table*. In the next chapter we will study the use of *records*, which store data as a list of *named attributes*.

□ ARRAY TYPE

Consider the drawing shown in Figure 10.2. It is made of seven points, six of which are connected by line segments. Each point is uniquely defined by a pair of X,Y coordinates, while each line segment is uniquely defined by its endpoints. Thus segment A is defined by points 1 and 2 that, in turn, are defined by the coordinate pairs (400,500) and (600,400), respectively.

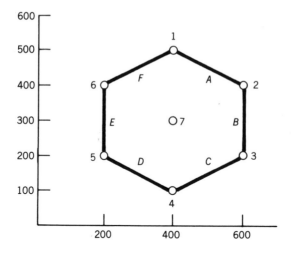

Figure 10.2. Storing a figure as a table of coordinate values.

It is easy to see how this figure can be stored in a pair of tables. The first table, which we will call POINTLIST, lists the X and Y values for each point:

POINTLIST	X	Y
1	400	500
2	600	400
3	600	200
4	400	100
5	200	200
6	200	400
7	400	300

The second table, which we will call LINELIST, stores for each line segment the numbers that identify its two endpoints:

LINELIST	First point	Second point
A	1	2
B	2	3
C	3	4
D	4	5
E	5	6
F	6	1

Note that each number in table LINELIST corresponds to a row of coordinate values in table POINTLIST. To draw line A, for example, we would use points 1 and 2, whose coordinates are (400,500) and (600,400), respectively.

It is easy to see how we can modify the drawing either by changing the location of individual points or by changing the relationship between them. This second option is depicted in Figure 10.3. While this change does not affect table POINTLIST, it completely revamps table LINELIST.

Indexed Sets

In mathematical terms, the tables representing Figures 10.2 and 10.3 are known as *indexed sets* of values. An indexed set of values is a set of ordered pairs (I,R). The first element of each pair is known as the *indexing value* or simply the *index*. The index comes from an ordered set, such as the integers or an enumerated type, and must be unique among the pairs that make up the indexed set—that is, no two pairs may have the same index. The second element of each ordered pair is a value from some designated type, for example CHAR, which we shall call the *base type*.

An indexed set defines a sequence of values of the base type. The ordering of the values is thus not determined by the values of the base type elements themselves, but rather by the progression of the indexing values.

Since each index is unique, we can refer to an element in the sequence by its index—point 3, line D, and so on. This ability to name values is a very powerful aid to computation since it makes it possible to access an element directly with-

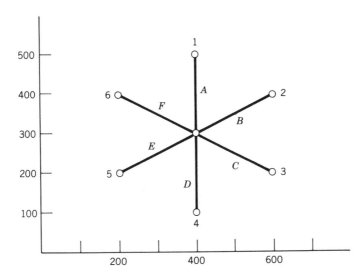

Figure 10.3. Changing the drawing by redefining the relationships between its constituent points.

out having to scan the entire list to find it. This is known as *random access*. It also makes it possible to change the value of a particular element without necessarily changing the whole set.

So that the computer can easily represent an indexed set, two constraints are imposed on it. One constraint is that all the elements of the set must be of the same base type. The second constraint is that the number of elements must be finite, which means that the index must have a finite domain. Type REAL may not be used for the index because the domain of REAL numbers is infinite. If INTEGER is used, then a finite subrange must be specified. Type CHAR and user-defined enumerated types have a finite domain and may, therefore, be used without restriction.

The base type of an indexed set can be any type that we choose—CHAR, REAL, INTEGER, or even another indexed set.

As implemented in Pascal, an indexed set is called an *array*. An array type is declared in terms of an *index* type and a *base* type.

The index type is specified within square brackets. It must be ordered and finite; the most common index type is a finite subrange of the integers.

The base type, which follows the keyword OF, can be any type at all. For example, a line of text can be represented as an array of characters, a vector can be represented as an array of numbers, and a matrix, which consists of several columns each of which is a vector, as an array of vectors. For example, the array declaration

```
type    list = array [1..26] of char;
var     alphabet : list;
```

sets up a data structure capable of holding 26 values of type CHAR. A particular set of such 26 values is shown in table ALPHABET.

ALPHABET	Character
1	'A'
2	'B'
3	'C'
.	.
.	.
26	'Z'

The letters in table ALPHABET are the data stored in the array, while the numbers are the ordinal value of their position in the list. Thus 'B' is in the second position, and 'Z' in the 26th position in the list. The list as a whole is called ALPHABET, which is a variable of type LIST.

The declaration of the array does not automatically fill it with the letters shown in table ALPHABET. It only provides the framework where such values can be stored. This framework must be filled cell by cell by the programmer. To assign 'A' to the first cell in the table, we must perform the following assignments:

```
alphabet[1] := 'A'
```

In this statement we refer to the table by its name ALPHABET and to a particular element in it by the index [1], which denotes the location of that element in the array.

The use of square brackets may seem confusing at first. In an array type declaration the square brackets are used to specify the *range* and *type* of the index. When we access an element of the array they are used to specify a *value* of the index. To avoid confusion, keep in mind that the first usage occurs only in declaration blocks; the second only in the body of the program.

Obviously, the sequence 'A', 'B', . . . 'Z' is only one of many possible contents of the array ALPHABET. We could fill all its cells with the letter 'A', or for that matter, with any value of type CHAR, including +, %, @, and any other symbol. There are only two restrictions that we must observe: We may fill the cells only with values of type CHAR, and we may only access cells whose index value is within the declared range. Attempting to assign a value to the 27th cell of ALPHABET, for instance, will cause a run-time error since no such cell exists. We must also be aware of the fact that assigning a new value to an existing cell erases the old content of that cell, just like any other assignment.

The individual cells in the array behave just like simple scalar variables. The only difference is that the cells of the array share a common name—in this case, ALPHABET. This may be likened to a family name, which by no means reduces the individuality of the members of the family. We can talk about the Brown family as a whole, or about Jim Brown as an individual who happens to belong to the Brown family. Likewise, the cell named ALPHABET[1] is a variable of type CHAR, but it is also part of a "family" of variables whose common name is ALPHABET. As an individual variable, ALPHABET[1] can be assigned to a scalar variable of type CHAR. For example,

```
type    list = array [1..26] of char;
var     alphabet : list;
        c         : char;

begin
  alphabet[1] := 'A';
  c := alphabet[1]
end;
```

The result of this simple sequence of assignments is that the scalar variable C now has the value 'A'.

As a "family," ALPHABET can be assigned to another variable of type LIST by means of a single assignment statement. For example,

```
type    list = array [1..26] of char;
var     alphabet, letters : list;

begin
  alphabet[1] := 'A';   (* assign individually *)
  alphabet[2] := 'B';
      .
      .
  alphabet[26] := 'Z';

  letters := alphabet (* assign as a whole *)
end;
```

This single assignment is equivalent to assigning each cell of the array variable ALPHABET individually to the corresponding cell of the array variable LETTERS (i.e., to a cell that has the same index value).

The Type of the Index

The type of the index of an array, as noted earlier, can be any ordered type in Pascal. In the above example we used a subrange of type INTEGER, specifically values 1 through 26 (denoted 1..26). We could, however, use other subranges of INTEGER, such as $-1..5$, or 27..36. Alternatively, we could use an enumerated type that we declared ourselves. This is a feature that is most useful for our purposes as programmers of graphic software. A point on the screen is a pair of coordinate values, X and Y. We could, therefore, make POINT an array of two cells, called X and Y, respectively, that can contain values of type integer:

```
type    coords = (x,y);
        point  = array [coords] of integer;
var     p      : point;

begin
  p[x] := 300;
  p[y] := 100
end;
```

In this example, COORDS is an enumerated type that consists of two values, X and Y. It serves as an index for the array type called POINT, so that POINT is a table of two cells that can be referred to by the names X and Y. Each cell can be assigned a value of type INTEGER.

Multidimensional Arrays

We can extend our definition of array types by taking advantage of the fact that the base type of an array can be any type in Pascal, including another array. The following example defines the Pascal data structure for a list of points like those depicted in Figures 10.2 and 10.3:

```
var   pointlist : array [1..7] of point;
```

Here POINT is itself an array, as defined above. This declaration is equivalent to the declaration

```
var   pointlist : array [1..7] of
                  array [coords] of integer;
```

or more compactly to

```
var   pointlist : array [1..7, coords] of integer;
```

Any one of these declarations is legal in Pascal, and they all define the same structure: a table of seven rows, indexed by the integer subrange 1..7, and two columns, indexed by the enumerated type (X,Y).

To store the shape depicted in Figure 10.2 in this structure, we must simply assign individual values to the various cells of the array variable POINTLIST:

```
pointlist[1,x] := 400;  pointlist[1,y] := 500;
pointlist[2,x] := 600;  pointlist[2,y] := 400;
  .
  .
```

Note that we now must specify both indices when addressing individual cells; otherwise our intended assignment might be ambiguous. For example, the variable POINTLIST[1] is the name of an entire *row* of array POINTLIST, including both the X and the Y columns. This feature provides a particularly convenient way to operate on arrays: We can assign points using one statement, instead of two. To assign coordinate values to point 7, for example, we could generate the point independently, then assign it as a whole to POINTLIST[7]:

```
var   pnt : point;

begin
  pnt[x] := 400; pnt[y] := 300;
  pointlist[7] := pnt
end;
```

The effect of these assignments is the same as that of

```
pointlist[7,x] := 400;   pointlist[7,y] := 300
```

Multidimensional arrays need not be restricted to two dimensions. For example, we could define LINE to be an array of *pairs* of points, and LINELIST to be an array of six lines:

```
type   line     = array [1..2] of point;
       linelist = array [a..f] of line;
```

This data structure defines a three-dimensional table, as depicted in Figure 10.4. The table consists of six levels, labeled A through F, each of which contains two points. Each point is made of two elements, X and Y. To address a single value (which is still of type INTEGER), we must provide three indices. For example, if we declare LINES to be a variable of type LINELIST:

```
var   lines : linelist
```

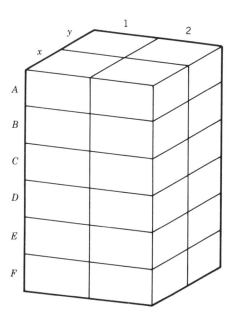

Figure 10.4. A three-dimensional table.

then the following statement can be used to assign the integer value 600 to the X coordinate of the second point of the first line in LINES. Note that the order of the subscripts in the assignment must match their order in the declaration part:

```
lines [a,2,x] := 600
```

Although there is no theoretical limit to the number of dimensions that can be assumed by an array data structure, there is a practical limit due to availability of memory space in the computer. A 10-dimensional array with only 10 units for each dimension requires memory space of 10 to the power of 10, which is 10,000,000,000 (10 billion) cells!

Operating on Arrays

Since the index that enables us to address the elements of an array is ordered, we can use such operators as FOR loops to compute the index and then operate directly on the corresponding array element. Suppose we have generated the shape depicted in Figure 10.2 and have stored it in an array variable LINES of type LINELIST. The stored shape can now be displayed by using Procedure DISPLAYSHAPE, which draws lines to the coordinates of the stored endpoints of each line.

If we now want to translate the shape by 300 units in the X direction and 200 units in the Y direction, we could use nested FOR loops to go through the list and increment the values stored in each cell without actually naming each cell separately. Procedure TRANSLATESHAPE performs this translation; its results for DX = 300 and DY = 200 are depicted in Figure 10.5.

Note that LINES is a VAR parameter because the procedure *changes* the val-

PROCEDURE DISPLAYSHAPE

```
procedure displayshape (lines : linelist);
(* displays list of lines stored in array lines *)

var    l : a..f;

begin
  for l := a to f do
    begin
      moveto (lines [l][1][x], lines [l][1][y]);
      drawto (lines [l][2][x], lines [l][2][y]);
    end
end;  (* of displayshape procedure *)
```

PROCEDURE TRANSLATESHAPE

```
procedure translateshape (var lines : linelist;
                          dx,dy : integer);
(* translates the 6 lines stored in array lines by
   dx in x direction, and dy in y direction *)

var   l : a..f;
      j : 1..2;

begin
  for l := a to f do
    for j := 1 to 2 do
      begin
        lines [l][j][x] := lines [l][j][x] + dx;
        lines [l][j][y] := lines [l][j][y] + dy
      end
end;  (* of translateshape procedure *)
```

PROCEDURE MOVESHAPE

```
procedure moveshape (var lines : linelist);
(* gets two points from user-input, and translates
   the lines stored in array linelist accordingly,
   then displays the shape in its new location. *)

var  dx,dy, x1,y1, x2,y2 : integer;

begin
  (* get user input of two points *)
  readln (x1,y1);
  readln (x2,y2);

  (* compute displacements in x and y *)
  dx := x2 - x1;
  dy := y2 - y1;

  translateshape (lines, dx,dy);
  displayshape (lines)
end; (* of moveshape procedure *)
```

ues it stores and because these changes must be communicated to the environment from which Procedure TRANSLATESHAPE is called.

We could write a more general procedure to perform any desired translation of shapes. All that is necessary is the means to get and compute the user-specified displacements in directions X and Y. Procedure MOVESHAPE performs this task.

Of course, there will now be *two* shapes on the screen—the old one and the new one, as depicted by Figure 10.5. If we wish to keep only the new shape, we must erase the old one. This can be accomplished by "undrawing" it, that is, by redrawing the old shape in the background color. Alternatively, this can be accomplished by clearing the screen before the new shape is drawn, by calling the external Procedure CLEARSCREEN, which is one of our graphics library routines.

Similar operators can now be embedded in our drafting package. They provide the benefits of storing each point registered by the user in an array data structure so that we can change the drawing without having to redraw it from scratch.

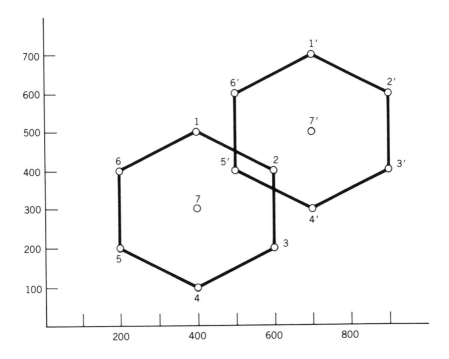

Figure 10.5. Translating a shape.

SUMMARY

We can use *data structures* to deal with collections of related values. The individual values or *elements* of a data structure may belong to one or more previously defined data types, called the *base* types.

An *array* is a data structure is composed of a fixed number of elements that are all of the same type. The elements are addressed by means of an *index*, which must be of a finite, ordered type. The base type of the elements can be any type, including another array.

A *multidimensional array* is an array whose base type is another array. To access an individual element of a multidimensional array we need one index for each dimension.

We can operate on arrays conveniently by using the index of the array as the loop control variable of a FOR loop, for example, thus performing some operation on all elements of the array.

11

RECORDS

In Chapter 10 we saw one way to store the graphic information generated on the screen, which was to use arrays. While convenient for many purposes, arrays are limited in that all their elements have to be of the same type. Furthermore, the restrictions imposed by Pascal on the indices of the array force us to express them as a subrange of INTEGER or as elements of an enumerated type.

These limitations seem to contradict what we said about data types in Chapter 9: They enable us to convey information in terms of the problem rather than the constraints of the programming language. To illustrate this point, consider how the following attributes of a line can be stored:

1. Two endpoints, in terms of their X,Y coordinates.
2. Color (red, green, blue).
3. Weight (light, medium, heavy).
4. Style (solid, broken).

We could, of course, express each one of these attributes as an integer, thus describing a line as follows:

LINE [752, 512, 314, 128, 1, 2, 1]

What does this collection of integers describe? A line with endpoints at (752,512) and (314,128), color red, weight medium, and style solid. It would be much easier for the reader to decipher the same line information if it were given as

```
LINE
    ENDPOINT [1] : [752,512];
    ENDPOINT [2] : [314,128];
    COLOR        : RED;
    WEIGHT       : MEDIUM;
    STYLE        : SOLID;
```

The number of attributes in this collection, like the elements of an array, is fixed; but unlike the elements of an array, they are of different types. We call this collection of attributes a *record*.

□ RECORD TYPE

Records, in the ordinary sense of the word, are used for describing real-world objects. The object to be described may be tangible, like a person, a building, or a ship; or it may be an abstract concept such as a bank account, a corporation, or a student's course grades. The record of an object usually contains only partial information about it—that which is pertinent to the intended data processing applications.

In Pascal, the RECORD data type is the most general structured type. By definition, it is a structured type with a predetermined number of components, each of which may be of different types. The components are called *fields,* and they are accessible through a set of selectors called *field names.*

The record type declaration describes how records of that type are to be constructed. We may think of it as a template that can be used to manufacture individual records. For example, we may define a LINE as a record type:

```
type   line = record
          endpoint : array [1..2, coords] of integer;
          color    : (red, green, blue);
          weight   : (light, medium, heavy);
          style    : (solid, broken)
       end;
```

This declaration sets up a template with seven fields, each of which can assume one value out of a range of possible values.

If we now declare L1 and L2 to be variables of type LINE, we can assign specific values to their field attributes, referring to them by name. For example,

```
var   l1,l2 : line;

begin
   l1.endpoint[1,x]  := 752;
   l1.endpoint[1,y]  := 512;
   l1.endpoint[2,x]  := 314;
   l1.endpoint[2,y]  := 128;
   l1.color          := red;
   l1.weight         := medium;
   l1.style          := solid
end;
```

To select a particular attribute, or field of the record variable, we write the name of the variable, then a dot (.), then the name of the field. For example, if we want to draw the line we have just created, we would use the following commands:

```
moveto(l1.endpoint[1,x],l1.endpoint[1,y]);
drawto(l1.endpoint[2,x],l1.endpoint[2,y])
```

Alternatively, we could assign the X and Y values to temporary integer variables X1,Y1,X2,Y2 and use them instead. For example,

```
x1 := l1.endpoint[1,x];   y1 := l1.endpoint[1,y];
x2 := l1.endpoint[2,x];   y2 := l1.endpoint[2,y];

moveto(x1,y1);
drawto(x2,y2)
```

Like an array variable, line L1 can be used as a "package" of information. Thus we can copy it to L2, another variable of type LINE:

```
l2 := l1
```

This assignment is equivalent to assigning the attribute values of L1 to L2 one by one. Again we see the analogy to first names and family names: L1 is the family name of the attributes by which we can refer to them collectively, while L1.END-POINT[1,X] is the name of one integer value, which is part of the L1 collection.

There are several similarities between record data types and array data types. Both are used to represent *N-tuples*—that is, a collection of N data elements. Both are random-access structures: Their components may be accessed directly and updated selectively. The *cardinality*, or number of elements, of both data types is the product of the cardinalities of their component types. For example, the LINE record defined earlier in this chapter is of cardinality 7, because its ENDPOINT field is an array that holds four values (an X,Y pair of integers for each one of its two endpoints), and one value for each of the other three fields (COLOR, WEIGHT, and STYLE).

The essential distinction between the two structured types is in the restrictions on the type of their components: While all the components of an array must be of the same type, the components of a record may have different types.

This distinction is reflected in the selection mechanisms for the two structured types. A computed selector (e.g., the FOR loop control variable) can be used to access elements of an array, but not to access elements of a record. Since there may be several different component types in a record, a computed selector—which depends on some data available only at execution time—might reference different components at different times, assigning different data types to a variable on different invocations. This would violate the restriction that Pascal imposes on all data types: The type of an element must be known by its syntax alone, without executing the program. To avoid this difficulty, an element of a record may be accessed only through an explicit field name. This implies that all field names within a record type must be unique.

Combined Array/Record Data Structures

We can now combine array and record types to form a data structure capable of representing and storing our drawings. In the LINE record, we have already seen a record type that contains an array as the type of one of its fields, for the purpose of storing the endpoints coordinates. Similarly, we can declare an *array of records* that combines into one array several LINE records of the type declared earlier:

```
var    linelist : array [1..20] of line;
```

This declaration sets up a structure comprising 20 line records. We can access a particular line record by referring to its ordinal number in LINELIST, then access its attributes by referring to their field names. For example, we can assign the color RED to the fifth line, using the statement

```
linelist[5].color := red
```

Similarly, to initialize all 20 lines to style SOLID, we can use a FOR loop:

```
for i := 1 to 20 do
   linelist[i].style := solid;
```

If we now want to display all lines that are green, we can use the following statements:

```
for i := 1 to 20 do
   if linelist[i].color = green
      then  begin
               moveto (linelist[i].endpoint[1,x],
                       linelist[i].endpoint[1,y]);
               drawto (linelist[i].endpoint[2,x],
                       linelist[i].endpoint[2,y])
            end;
```

The WITH Statement

It is often necessary to access different components of the same record several times in a small section of the program, as in the last example. This situation arises from the very nature of a structured data type since we deal with variables whose components are logically related. Unfortunately, the components of a record cannot be processed concisely, as can the components of an array, by using the repetition statement FOR. This is precluded by the diversity of the component types in a record and the need to name them explicitly, as we discussed earlier. It is necessary, then, to provide a different shorthand mechanism for processing records. This mechanism is called the WITH statement: It lets us access the components of a record as if they were simple variables, by removing the record variable name and referring directly to the field name. For example, we could simplify the last example by applying the WITH statement:

```
for i := 1 to 20 do
   with linelist[i] do
      if color = green
         then  begin
                  moveto (endpoint[1,x], endpoint[1,y]);
                  drawto (endpoint[2,x], endpoint[2,y])
               end;
```

This sequence of statements has exactly the same effect as the former. The only difference is that we have separated the "family name" LINELIST[I] from the "first names" COLOR and ENDPOINT by means of the WITH statement. The WITH statement tells the compiler that from here until the end of the statement, all the record components that are used belong to the particular record variable that is named in the body of the WITH statement.

Despite its usefulness, the WITH statement should be used cautiously. Indiscriminate use can lead to confusing and ambiguous programs in which the compiler may interpret the statements differently from what you expected.

☐ SUMMARY

In order to store a collection of data about a real-world object and convey the information in terms of the object itself, it is often convenient to use *records*.

A *record* is a structured data type composed of a fixed number of elements, each of which may be of a different type. The components are called *fields* and can be accessed only by explicit reference to their *field names*.

The WITH statement is a shorthand mechanism that enables us to access several fields of one record variable without specifying the variable name each time.

12

POINTERS

So far we have studied several data types that can be used to store the information generated on the screen by the user: scalar types, arrays, and records. These data types are quite useful, but they are rather rigid in that the number of elements we wish to store must be declared ahead of time. For an interactive graphic program this is a serious flaw. The programmer must decide in advance that the program will be capable of drawing, say, up to 5000 lines; and this number has to be written in the program before the user can draw the first line. If the user wants to add the 5001st line, the data structure will be unable to accommodate it. If, on the other hand, the user draws only 10 lines, then 4990 storage spaces have been wasted.

Clearly, in a situation when the programmer cannot predict the number of elements the user will want to store, it is desirable to construct a data structure that can grow and shrink as the drawing develops, that is, at run time. We call such structures *dynamic structures.*

The virtue of dynamic structures is their ability to grab and release storage space on demand. In other words, run-time demand, rather than compile-time prediction, determines how much storage (memory cells) are used by the program. The amount of storage changes throughout the execution of the program.

With scalar types, arrays, and records, every memory cell used by the program is associated with a name that is declared in the body of the program. In other words, each cell is associated with an entity that exists at compile time. Given this one-to-one relationship, how can the program use more memory cells than have been associated with its declared variables? That is, how can the program use memory cells that do not have explicit names at compile time?

Clearly, we cannot associate dynamically allocated memory cells with the static names that are declared in the body of the program. But recall from Chapter 2 that the names we use in the program are only convenient high-level identifiers for the machine addresses of the memory cells that the program actually uses. These names provide the programmer with an English-like representation for otherwise awkward and machine-dependent symbols. If we could access these machine addresses directly, we could use the memory cells they denote without using high-level names that must be declared in the body of the program at compile time. If, in addition, we could "grab" new memory cells on demand, we would have the desired dynamic memory management capabilities.

□ POINTER TYPE

Given that Pascal provides us with a mechanism to allocate and release memory cells at run time, as we shall see later, the problem of dynamic allocation of memory cells is transformed into finding other, possibly indirect means to access these cells, means that do not require static compile-time declarations.

Pascal provides us with such means. It allows us to store the *machine address* of memory cells as a value of some static variables. This kind of variables belong to a data type that is different in principle from those we have seen before. Called a *pointer type,* the values that comprise its domain are the machine addresses of other memory cells, rather than terminal values such as integers and reals.

Figure 12.1 depicts two memory cells of different types. The one on the right stores a value of type INTEGER. The one on the left stores a value of type POINTER-TO-INTEGER; that is, the machine address of a cell capable of storing values of type INTEGER. Such pointer values are commonly represented by arrows since they "point" at other cells.

Pointers—also known as references—are one of the most important and powerful features of any programming language that employs them. At the same time, they are one of the most subtle and dangerous features to use. They allow the programmer to construct arbitrary data structures that are essential to the design of good problem-specific programs. Unfortunately, they can also be misused to construct unnecessarily complex and "fragile" data structures that are hard to understand. Like any powerful tool, pointers must be used with care and restraint.

We can declare a pointer type for any data type in Pascal. The pointer type is denoted by prefixing the up-arrow symbol (^) to the base type. Thus we may have a variable of type ^INTEGER (which we read as POINTER-TO-INTEGER), the

Figure 12.1. A pointer variable.

value of which is the address of a memory cell capable of storing an INTEGER value:

```
type    ptr = ^integer;
var     ref : ptr;
```

The value of REF is not of type INTEGER (such as 5 or 37), but rather the *address* of another memory cell, which in turn can be assigned a value of type INTEGER.

To emphasize its role as a pointer to another memory cell, we will customarily depict a pointer data structure by an arrow emanating from the pointer variable and leading to a box that represents the memory cell referenced by that pointer. The pointer REF is depicted in Figure 12.2.

A pointer variable may be used in the following ways:

1. It may be assigned; that is, we may assign it a value, and it may be assigned to another variable of the same type.
2. It may be passed as a parameter to functions and procedures, and it can be returned as a value of a function.
3. It may be tested for equality or inequality.
4. It may be used to access a memory cell that has not been associated with a declared variable at compile time, but has been allocated dynamically during run time.

The domain of values for a pointer variable includes the machine addresses of all cells that may contain a variable of the pointer's base type. It also includes the value NIL that indicates that the pointer variable does not point to any usable value. NIL, a reserved word in Pascal, is usually used to indicate the end of a list. It is denoted in diagrams by the electrical "ground" symbol.

Dereferencing Pointers

Besides equality and assignment, the principle operation associated with pointer variables is *dereferencing*. The dereference operator accepts a pointer value and returns the value that is stored in the memory cell referenced by that pointer.

Figure 12.2. Graphic representation of a pointer variable.

The dereferencing operator is denoted by postfixing the up-arrow symbol (^) to the pointer variable identifier. If X is a variable of type INTEGER, and REF is a variable of type POINTER-TO-INTEGER, then we can dereference REF and assign the result to X:

```
x := ref^
```

We read this as "REF dereferenced" or "REF follow-the-arrow."

The up-arrow notation may seem confusing at first since it is used for two different purposes:

1. To *declare* a pointer type or a pointer variable.
2. To *dereference* a pointer variable.

To avoid confusion, keep in mind that to declare a pointer type or variable, we *prefix* the up-arrow to a *type* identifier (^INTEGER); this occurs only in declaration blocks. To dereference a pointer variable, as in an assignment statement or parameter, we *postfix* the up-arrow to a *variable* identifier (REF^); this occurs only in the body of the program itself.

The Use of Pointers in Assignments

The assignment operator works in essentially the same way for pointer variables as it does for scalars, array elements, and record fields. But there are some necessary adaptations for each of these cases.

Suppose we apply the assignment operator to a scalar variable:

```
x := y + 1
```

The left-hand side of the assignment statement is the identifier for a variable; that is, for a memory cell capable of storing a value of a certain type. The right-hand side is an expression that yields a value of that type. We replace the value currently associated with the left-hand side variable by the value of the expression on the right-hand side of the assignment statement.

When we apply the assignment operator to an element of an array, we find that the left-hand side is not the identifier for a memory cell. Rather, it is an *expression* that must be evaluated in order to find the address of a particular memory cell, as in the following example:

```
a[7] := 38
```

We evaluate A[7] to obtain the address of the seventh element of the array called A. We can then store the value 38 at that address.

To make an assignment to a field of a record, we again must evaluate the left-hand side:

```
l.color := red
```

Here we obtain the address of the field named COLOR in record L and store the value RED in that address.

With pointer variables, one of two distinct assignment operations can be performed, depending whether the left-hand side of the assignment statement contains the pointer variable itself (REF) or the *dereferenced* pointer variable (REF^).

In the first case, where we assign to REF itself, the assignment operation behaves just like an assignment to a scalar variable. The left-hand side of the statement is the identifier of a memory cell; the right-hand side is a value that can be stored in that cell. To perform the assignment, we simply replace the current content of the cell with the new value. Since the identifier happens to be a pointer variable, the value represents the address of some other memory cell.

The second case, where we assign to REF^, is more like assigning to an element of an array or a field of a record. The left-hand side of the statement is not the identifier of a memory cell, but an expression that must be evaluated to determine a memory address. We evaluate it by dereferencing; that is, we read the *contents* of REF to determine the *physical location in memory* of REF^. We then store the value of the expression on the right-hand side in that memory cell.

Consider the following cases. We will use two simple variables, V and W, of type REAL, and two pointer variables R and S that are of type ^REAL (POINTER-TO-REAL). Let us assume that initially R points to V; that is, it contains the memory address of V, and S points to W. This is depicted in Figure 12.3*a*.

Let us now perform the following assignment on the variables depicted in Figure 12.3*a*:

```
r := s
```

The resulting relationships are depicted in Figure 12.3*b*. The variable called R has been assigned the value of the variable called S. But what is this value? It is the *memory address* of W. So now R contains the memory address of W, as does S; we show this fact by drawing an arrow from R to W.

Now suppose that we go back to the original memory map shown in Figure 12.3*a*, and perform the following operation instead:

```
r^ := s^
```

The result is quite different, as depicted in Figure 12.3*c*. The value stored at the memory address that is *referenced by R*, that is, the *value of V*, has been

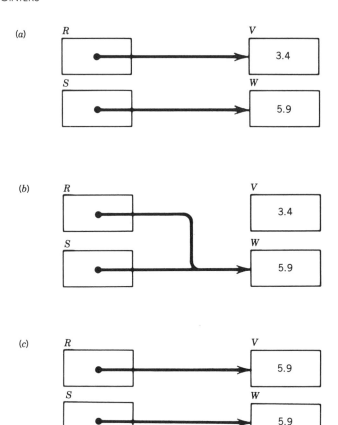

Figure 12.3. (*a*) Initial partial memory map; (*b*) after R := S; (*c*) after R^ := S^.

changed. It is now equal to the value stored at the memory address that is *referenced by S;* that is, the *value of W.* The value of R itself, which is the address of V, has not been changed!

The effects of these two different assignment operations can be seen if we now change the value of W, say by

```
W := 7.3
```

In the situation depicted by Figure 12.3*b,* the evaluation of R^ will now yield the new value (7.3), and so will the evaluation of S^, because *both R and S point to W.* On the other hand, in the situation depicted by Figure 12.3*c,* while the evaluation of S^ will yield the *new value* (7.3), the evaluation of R^ will still yield the *old value* (5.9) because *there is no connection between R and W*.

This kind of distinction is particularly important when we use dynamic structures for graphics. Suppose that we have created the following data structure for points and lines:

```
type   coords = (x,y);
       point  = array [coords] of integer;
       ptr    = ^point;
       line   = array [1..2] of ptr;
```

A POINT, in this data structure, is an array of two integer values (indexed by the enumerated type COORDS); PTR is a POINTER-TO-POINT; and a LINE is an array of PTRs. Thus the data structure for each LINE contains the addresses of two memory units, each capable of holding an integer value.

Using this data structure, let us store the data for the assembly of lines depicted in Figure 12.4*a*. Of course, there are many ways we could represent this assembly. Suppose that each one of the six lines contains a PTR pointing to the *same* POINT; that is, the same memory cells, containing one pair of X,Y coordinates (a situation that is similar to that depicted by Figure 12.3*b*). If we now change the value of those coordinates, the image will change drastically, as in Figure 12.4*b*, since all six lines are affected.

Suppose, instead, that the situation in Figure 12.3*c* occurs: The six lines have PTRs pointing to *six distinct* POINTs that happen to contain the same X,Y values. Now if we change the coodinate values for one POINT, the image is changed only slightly, as in Figure 12.4*d*, since only one of the six lines is affected.

□ POINTER SWINGING

It is often necessary to manipulate both the pointers to memory cells and the contents of those cells. Suppose that we want to transform the configuration shown in Figure 12.5*a* into the one shown in Figure 12.5*c*.

How can we perform this transformation? Clearly we must manipulate both the pointers to the cells and the contents of the cells. It will be easier to change the contents first, using simple assignment statements to arrive at Figure 12.5*b*. Then we will manipulate the pointers using a series of statements known as *pointer swinging* to arrive at Figure 12.5*c*.

The contents of the cell referenced by R must be swapped with the contents of the cell referenced by T. As we have seen in the SWAP programs of a previous chapter, swapping requires using a temporary variable; otherwise, the original

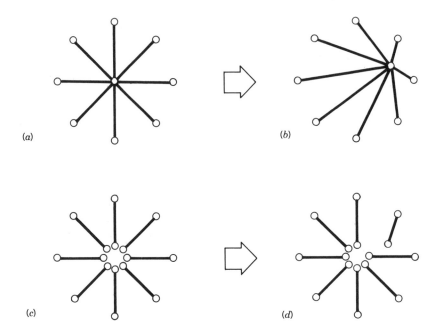

Figure 12.4. (*a*) Initial image; (*b*) result when pointers share a vertex; (*c*) result when pointers do not share.

value of the first variable will be lost when we assign to it the value of the second variable. Here we will use a temporary variable of the same type as X and Y to store the *contents* of the cell referenced by R:

```
vtmp := r^
```

Now we find the contents of the cell referenced by T and assign it to the cell referenced by R:

```
r^ := t^
```

We complete the swap by assigning the value of the temporary variable VTMP to the cell referenced by T:

```
t^ := vtmp
```

Now we take the content of the second cell and add it to the content of the cell reference by T:

```
t^ := t^ + s^
```

(a)

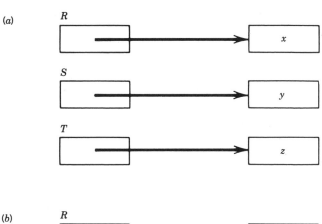

(b)

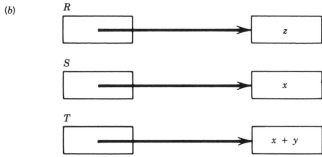

(c)

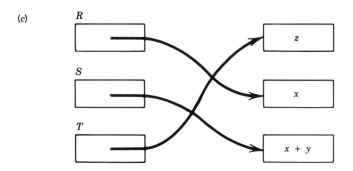

Figure 12.5. (*a*) Initial memory map; (*b*) after manipulating contents; (*c*) after pointer swinging.

We have arrived at Figure 12.5*b* and can proceed to swing the pointers themselves. Here again we need a temporary variable—in this case, a temporary *pointer variable,* PTMP. We find the *value of R* which is, of course, the address of some other cell, and assign it to PTMP:

```
ptmp := r
```

This step is illustrated in Figure 12.6*a*. Now we swing the pointer R by finding the value of S and assigning it to R; that is, we make R point to the same address that S points to:

```
r := s
```

This step is illustrated in Figure 12.6*b*. Similarly, we swing pointer S (Figure 12.6*c*):

```
s := t
```

Finally, we swing pointer T (Figure 12.6*d*):

```
t := ptmp
```

The end result is the configuration of Figure 12.5*c*, which is what we set out to accomplish.

Note that we have operated on "nameless" memory cells by means of manipulating the named pointer variables. The ability to operate on nameless memory cells is the key to the power of the pointer type, which enables us to access variables that were generated dynamically during run time.

☐ DYNAMIC MEMORY ALLOCATION

Memory cells can be allocated dynamically by means of the standard Pascal procedure NEW. This procedure has the form of:

```
new(p)
```

in which the argument P is a pointer to some type T:

```
var p : ^t;
```

Procedure NEW performs two actions:

1. It allocates a memory cell that is able to store a variable of type T from an area of Pascal storage called the "heap."

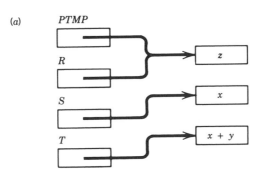

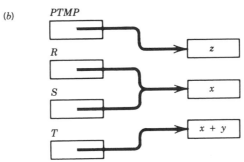

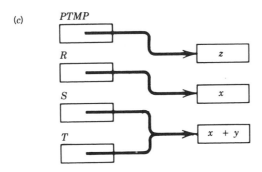

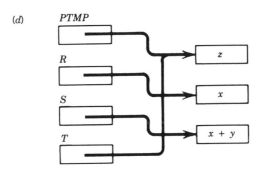

Figure 12.6. Pointer swinging.

Before: P

After: P

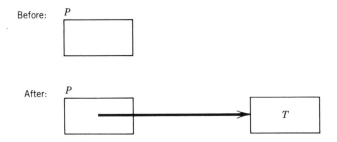

T

Figure 12.7. Allocating a new storage location.

2. It assigns to the argument P the address of this cell; that is, a value of type POINTER-TO-T, so that the cell may be accessed through P.

The result of NEW(P) is depicted in Figure 12.7.

Dynamic Memory Deallocation

Dynamic memory allocation is a very powerful tool. If not used with restraint, it can quickly allocate all the memory of a computer and thereby bring the execution of the program to a halt. The programmer who uses dynamic memory allocation must, therefore, also assume responsibility for releasing that memory when it is no longer needed. The command that performs this task is

```
dispose(p)
```

which does the opposite of NEW(P): It returns the memory cell to the heap and erases the value stored in P. It leaves P with no value at all!

☐ SUMMARY

If the lines of a drawing are to be stored in a static data structure, such as scalars, arrays, or records, we must decide in advance how many lines the data structure can hold. This is inconvenient, for we cannot know how large a drawing the user may wish to create.

A *dynamic structure* can grow or shrink as needed during the execution of the program. This is accomplished by means of *pointer types*.

A *pointer variable* contains the machine address of a memory cell. It is declared as type ^T, or POINTER-TO-T, where T can be any data type.

We can *assign* one pointer variable to another (R := S), provided that the two variables are pointers to the same data type. This assignment means that both pointers now reference the same memory cell.

We can *dereference* a pointer variable (R^), which yields the value contained in the memory cell referenced by the pointer.

We can also *assign a value* to a dereferenced pointer variable (R^ := X), provided that the value is of the type the pointer references. This assignment means that the cell referenced by the pointer now contains the new value.

The standard procedure NEW(P) allocates a new memory cell, and returns a pointer to that cell. This cell has not been associated with a declared variable in the program at compile time. It has, therefore, no name, and can be accessed only through the pointer P, which is the argument of procedure NEW. The new memory cell can store a value of the base type of the argument P.

The standard procedure DISPOSE releases the memory cell and leaves the pointer with no value.

13

LISTS

Now that we have studied the nature of pointer types, we can apply them for our purpose of storing the lines drawn by a user on the screen during a session with the program. We saw earlier how the data concerning a single line (endpoints, color, weight, style) can be stored in a record. We also saw that multiple records can be stored in an array. This structure was convenient, but it did not give us the flexibility to store a drawing containing many lines or, at the user's option, store a drawing containing few lines, without wasting the system's resources. How can the dynamic structuring capabilities of pointers give us the flexibility we desire?

A pointer type can be declared for any type in Pascal, including record types. We may, therefore, declare a record that has the following structure:

```
type   item = record
                 x,y  : integer;
                 link : ^item
              end;
var   list : ^item;
```

One of the attributes (fields) of this ITEM record is a pointer to a record of type ITEM itself. Utilizing this simple record, we can create a structure known as a linked list, which is depicted in Figure 13.1.

□ LINKED LISTS

As the name implies, and as depicted in Figure 13.1, a *linked list* is a structure made of elements connected by links. The elements of the list are all of some type ITEM; the links are represented by pointer variables of type ^ITEM. The list as a whole is accessible through a static pointer variable (LIST, in this example),

List

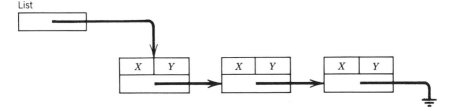

Figure 13.1. A linked list data structure.

which is also of type ^ITEM. We call it the *header* of the list. The last link is a pointer to NIL, which indicates that there are no other elements in the list.

What are the advantages of this kind of structure over an array? Linked lists have two important properties that arrays do not have:

1. The length of a linked list does not have to be determined at compilation time. Rather, the list can grow and shrink dynamically, as required by run-time conditions. For example, in a graphic program the structure may grow as the user adds lines and shrink as lines are deleted.
2. Linked lists are easy to manipulate; that is, addition and deletion of elements in the middle of the list is a simple matter. By contrast, deleting elements in the middle of an array leaves gaps in the structure that have to be managed.

Do not let the simplicity of type ITEM mislead you: The record may have any number of fields. It can still be linked to other records of the same type, provided that at least one of these fields is of type "pointer-to-the-record." For example, we can "link-list" the LINE record that we used earlier by adding a field called LINK:

```
type   line = record
          endpoint : array [1..2, coords] of integer;
          color    : (red, green, blue);
          weight   : (light, medium, heavy);
          style    : (solid, broken);
          link     : ^line
       end;
```

For the sake of simplicity, we will use the type ITEM declared above since we will be concerned here mostly with the LINK field of the record rather than its other fields.

To facilitate the use of this field, we will declare ^ITEM as a named type in its own:

```
type   itemptr = ^item;
```

and use this type in the declaration of type ITEM itself:

```
type  item = record
                 x,y  : integer;
                 link : itemptr
             end;
```

The declaration of ITEMPTR must, as we have seen so far in Pascal, precede its use. Thus in order for us to use it in the declaration of record ITEM—as the type of field LINK—the declaration of ITEMPTR must appear before the record it references has been declared! This case is similar to the case of declaring mutually recursive procedures that we saw in Chapter 7 and that was solved through forward referencing. Similarly, pointer types may be declared *before* their base types are declared. This is the only exception to the rule that type declarations must always precede their use.

Building Linked Lists

How is a linked list initialized, and how does it grow and shrink?

Initialization is done simply by setting the header of the list to NIL, denoting that the list is empty:

```
list := nil
```

Adding elements to the list is somewhat more involved. We must first allocate a memory space to accommodate the new element, using procedure NEW. Once allocated, we must attach the new element to the list. There are many different ways in which this attachment can be made. The simplest and most effective one is to add the element at the beginning of the list, so that it is referenced immediately by the header LIST, as depicted in Figure 13.2. Note that LIST is the only variable that is *declared* in the program. It is used to access the elements in the list, by pointing to the first element. All other elements are accessed by the LINK fields of their predecessors.

As is evident from Figure 13.2, existing elements get "pushed" further away from the header LIST as the structure grows. A sequence of statements that adds elements to the structure is shown in Procedure ADDELEMENT.

The first statement in the body of Procedure ADDELEMENT allocates a new record of type ITEMPTR. It assigns the address of this record to the temporary pointer variable TEMP.

The next two statements store the new X and Y values in the new record. To do this, we must first access the record by dereferencing TEMP; the up-arrow (^) denotes that TEMP is to be dereferenced. Then we can select the appropriate fields of the record. Using the same selection process we used for a field of a simple record, we append the record variable name with a dot (.), followed by the desired field name. In this case, the record name is TEMP^ so we write

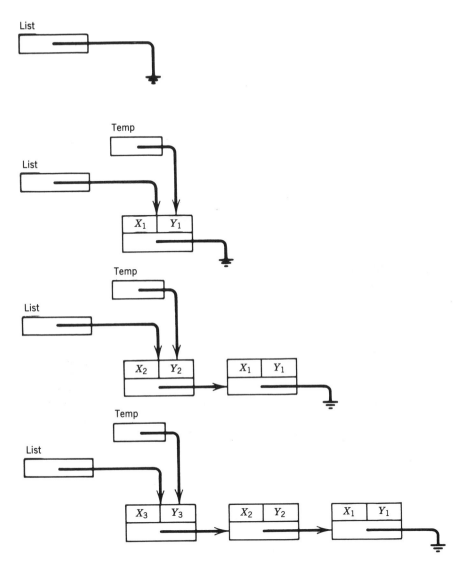

Figure 13.2. Adding elements to a linked list.

TEMP^.X to select its X field and TEMP^.Y to select its Y field. We can now assign the values XNEW and YNEW to the appropriate fields of the new record.

The next statement in Procedure ADDELEMENT assigns a value to the LINK field of TEMP:

```
temp^.link := list
```

PROCEDURE ADDELEMENT

```
procedure addelement (var list : itemptr;
                          xnew,ynew : integer);
(* adds a new element to list, setting its x and y
   fields to xnew and ynew, respectively *)

var  temp : itemptr;

begin
  (* allocate space for new element *)
  new(temp);

  (* assign values to it's X,Y fields *)
  temp^.x := xnew;
  temp^.y := ynew;

  (* connect new element to the list *)
  temp^.link := list;
  list := temp
end;   (* of addelement procedure *)
```

We access the LINK field just as we accessed the X and Y fields of the record. Then the value currently stored in LIST is assigned to LINK. Since LINK and LIST are pointer variables, that value is the machine address of the memory cell that contains the first element of the list. If the list is empty, the value assigned to LINK is NIL.

In the last statement of Procedure ADDELEMENT, the value currently stored in TEMP is assigned to LIST. LIST, a pointer variable, is the header of the list; and the value assigned to it is the machine address of the new record referenced by TEMP. Thus the new element becomes first in the list.

Successive invocations of Procedure ADDELEMENT will create a linked list of any desired length. For example, three invocations with the arguments (X1,Y1), (X2,Y2), and (X3,Y3) will generate the data structure depicted by Figure 13.2.

Traversing Linked Lists

Now that the list exists, what can we do with it? How can we, for example, go through the list and retrieve the elements stored in it, if the only element that can be accessed readily is the first one, and all the other elements are nameless?

The answer is found in a process known as *traversal*. We construct a temporary pointer variable that starts at the beginning of the list and "moves" from one element to the next until it reaches the end of the list. While pointing at an element, it provides direct access to all its fields. Procedure DISPLAYLIST performs a list traversal, drawing lines as it goes.

The most important statement in this procedure is:

```
temp := temp^.link
```

that advances the pointer TEMP to the next element in the list, as depicted in Figure 13.3.

Procedure DISPLAYLIST will draw the lines in the reverse order they were drawn by the user because the last line to be stored in the list is the first one encountered in the traversal. This order is known as *LIFO*-last in, first out. For most purposes this reverse order is of no consequence. However, if it is of consequence, we can build the list so that the first element stored in the list will be the first one encountered. This order is *FIFO*—first in, first out.

Hit Testing: Picking Graphic Elements on the Screen

List traversal can also be used to search for and find an element in the list that meets certain criteria. A useful application of this utility is to find an element whose X,Y coordinates match a screen location indicated by the user. We call this operation *hit testing* because we test each line to see if it is the one that the user "hit." Hit testing provides us with the means to "pick" an element that is displayed on the screen by simply pointing to it with the cursor. Once found, we can apply to that element certain operations, such as deleting it or moving it around. Function FINDELEMENT performs this search. It returns a pointer to

PROCEDURE DISPLAYLIST

```
procedure displaylist (list : itemptr);
(* traverses list and draws a line to each point
   it stores, except the first one *)

var   temp : itemptr;

begin
  temp := list;
  while temp <> nil do
    begin
      if temp = list
        then moveto(temp^.x, temp^.y)
        else drawto(temp^.x, temp^.y);

      temp := temp^.link
    end
end;  (* of displaylist procedure *)
```

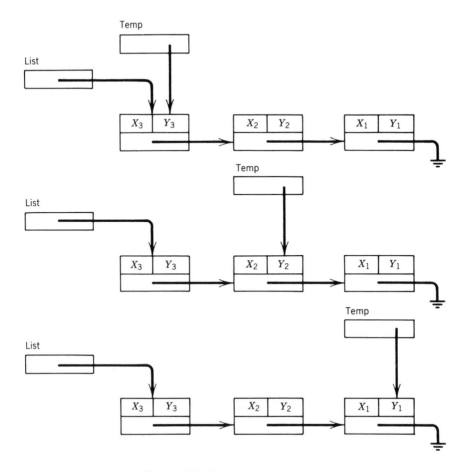

Figure 13.3. Traversing a linked list.

the element if found, or NIL if there is no element that matches the indicated screen location.

Note that Function FINDELEMENT utilizes a WHILE loop that advances the search pointer TEMP only if the location of the element that TEMP references in the list *does not* match the user-defined point on the screen. Otherwise, the boolean variable STOP is set to TRUE, which causes the loop to terminate. The loop will also terminate when TEMP = NIL—a condition that becomes true when TEMP has tested all the elements in the list but did not find one that matches the user-indicated screen location.

In fact, it is very difficult for a user to indicate the exact screen location of an element by pointing to it with the cursor. Therefore we usually provide a small

FUNCTION FINDELEMENT

```
function findelement (list : itemptr;
                      cx,cy : integer) : itemptr;
(* reads  user-defined  point  on the screen and
   returns pointer to the element in list one of
   whose endpoints matches that point *)

var    temp  : itemptr;
       stop  : boolean;

begin
  temp := list;      (* initialize search pointer *)
  stop := false;            (* set termination flag *)

  (* search *)
  while not stop and (temp <> nil) do
    if (temp^.x = cx) and (temp^.y = cy)
      then  stop := true
      else  temp := temp^.link;

  findelement := temp
end; (* of findelement function *)
```

range, or distance from the cursor, within which we consider the pick to be successful. We can implement this range by replacing the condition

```
(temp^.x = cx) and (temp^.y = cy)
```

with

```
(abs(temp^.x - cx) < range) and
(abs(temp^.y - cy) < range)
```

where RANGE is the permissible margin of error.

Deleting Elements from the List

Suppose we wish to delete an erroneous line or point from the list. We must first remove the element from the list and then release the memory cell it occupied by means of the DISPOSE routine.

There are two ways of removing an element from a linked list: one way for the first element in the list, and the other way for all the rest.

To remove the first element—that is, the element that is referenced by the pointer LIST itself—we must swing LIST to point to the successor of the first element, as depicted in Figure 13.4.

By swinging the pointer we make the first element inaccessible to LIST, thus loosing the ability to dispose of it. Therefore we must place a temporary pointer to that element before it is removed. Procedure DELETEFIRST performs this task.

This sequence of statements will fail if the list is empty to begin with. Therefore, we must first test whether the list is empty, and avoid the operation completely if it is.

To delete any element other than the first one in the list, we swing the LINK pointer of its *predecessor* element to point to its *successor,* a "bypass" that is depicted in Figure 13.5.

To perform a bypass we must first identify and have access to the predecessor of the element to be deleted. Assuming that we have a pointer to the element itself (otherwise, how would we know that it is the one to be deleted?), we can perform a *search,* starting with the first element, until we find an element whose LINK field points to the element to be deleted. This is the predecessor. Once we find the predecessor, we can remove and delete the element much as we did in Procedure DELETEFIRST: We swing the LINK pointer of the predecessor from the element that is to be deleted to its successor, then DISPOSE of the element. The bypass operation is implemented in Procedure DELETEELEMENT.

Parameter I in Procedure DELETEELEMENT is a pointer to the element that is to be removed. Finding the predecessor of the element that is referenced by I is performed by the first two statements. The first statement initializes a pointer variable called TEMP to reference the first element in the list. The second statement is a WHILE loop that moves this pointer along the elements of the list until it finds the predecessor of the element referenced by I.

PROCEDURE DELETEFIRST

```
procedure deletefirst (var list : itemptr);
(* removes and disposes first element in list *)

var    temp : itemptr;

begin
   temp := list;     (* assign temporary pointer *)
   list := temp^.link;    (* bypass first elemet *)

   dispose(temp)              (* dispose of temp *)
end;  (* of deletefirst procedure *)
```

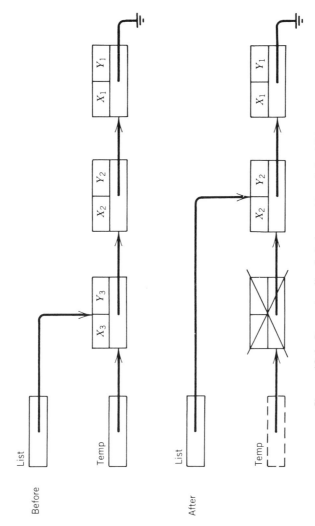

Figure 13.4. Removing the first element in a linked list.

How do we know that we have found the predecessor of the element in the list that is referenced by I? The test condition for the WHILE loop is

```
temp^.link <> i
```

TEMP is our temporary pointer, and TEMP^ is the element that it references. The LINK field is the pointer from TEMP^ to the next element in the list. The test condition is that the value of LINK is *not equal* to the value of I, the pointer to the element that we are trying to delete. If the two pointers are equal—that is, they contain the same address—then they point to the same memory cell. When we find an element whose LINK field is *equal* to I, it is the predecessor. While this condition is *not* true, we advance TEMP to its successor:

```
temp := temp^.link
```

and try again.

The third statement of Procedure DELETEELEMENT causes the pointer in the LINK field of TEMP to bypass I and point to its successor, thereby removing I from the list. The last two statements dispose of I and set it to NIL.

PROCEDURE DELETEELEMENT

```
procedure deleteelement (list  : itemptr;
                         var i : itemptr);
(* removes and disposes of element i in list *)

var   temp : itemptr;

begin
  (* find predecessor of i^ *)
  temp := list;
  while temp^.link <> i do
    temp := temp^.link;

  temp^.link := i^.link;        (* bypass i^      *)
  dispose(i);    i := nil       (* dispose of i^ *)
end;  (* of deleteelement procedure *)
```

Sorting with Linked Lists

To summarize the operations on linked lists, let us consider one of their uses: sorting a list of points.

Sorting is an important process by which elements of a list are arranged in order of some value. If a list containing the integers 3,2,5,1,4 is sorted in order of the values, it will become 1,2,3,4,5.

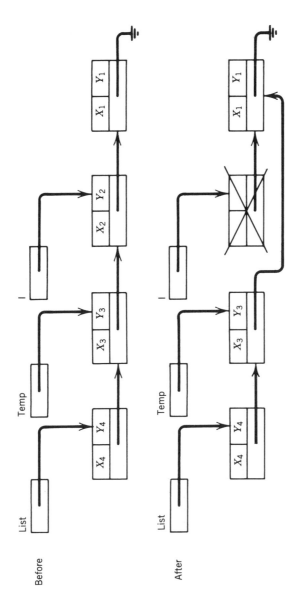

Figure 13.5. Removing an element of a linked list.

STEP	UNSORTED LIST					SORTED LIST				
0	3	2	5*	1	4			Empty		
1	3	2	1	4*						5
2	3*	2	1						4	5
3	2*	1						3	4	5
4	1*						2	3	4	5
5	Empty					1	2	3	4	5

Figure 13.6. Sorting a list.

There are many sorting algorithms, some more efficient than others. A very simple (and also inefficient) sorting algorithm is as follows:

1. Find the largest element in the unsorted list.
2. Remove it from the unsorted list.
3. Insert it as the first element in a new (sorted) list.
4. Repeat steps 1 through 3 until the unsorted list is empty.

This algorithm is illustrated in Figure 13.6. The element with an asterisk (*) is the current largest element in the unsorted list. Procedure SORTLIST on page 166–167 (which includes a number of nested routines) implements this algorithm for a list of points. It sorts them by their X values.

☐ OTHER LINEAR STRUCTURES

There are many variations on the linked list concept that are useful in specific applications. Among them are circular lists, doubly linked lists, and rings. In this chapter we will only mention a few of them and will not go into much detail in their description. The second volume of this series discusses such structures in great detail.

Circular Lists

In a *circular linked list* the last element points to the first element of the list, rather than NIL. An example of a circular list is shown in Figure 13.7.

This structure simplifies some operations, such as deleting a particular element. Instead of having one operator for the first element and a different operator for the rest, as is required for NIL-ended lists, the circular list can use the same operator to handle all the elements. Furthermore, we can use the header of the list for traversal or search instead of creating a temporary pointer.

It is convenient to add new elements in a circular list at the *second place,* rather than at the beginning of the list. This means that a new element will not be the first to be referenced by the header, but rather the second element (in other words, the header will point to the *predecessor* of the new element). As such, it is important to note the differences between adding the *first element to an empty list* and adding all other elements. Adding the first element to an empty list actually *creates* the list because an empty list cannot be circular. It thus involves the act of closing the circle (by making the first element point to itself), in addition to adding it to the list. Also, we must pay close attention to termination of list traversal since evaluation to NIL no longer works.

Doubly Linked Lists

The linking techniques described so far allow us to process the list in one direction only. In order to operate on the predecessor of an element in the list we must use a rather cumbersome technique, as seen in Procedure SORTLIST.

A *doubly linked list* makes it easy to move in the list in both directions. This structure has two links for each element, as depicted in Figure 13.8.

The appropriate record declaration now becomes

```
type   item = record;
               x,y           : integer;
               link1,link2 : itemptr
             end;
```

Adding and deleting elements in a doubly linked list is somewhat more involved, because we have to swing two pointers for each element rather than one, as depicted in Figure 13.8.

Rings

A doubly linked list can be made circular by connecting each end pointer to the element at the opposite end. This creates a structure called a *ring,* depicted in Figure 13.9.

This structure simplifies some of the operations on doubly linked lists, particularly if we define the empty ring to be a ring with a single dummy component linked to itself, as depicted in Figure 13.10.

☐ NONLINEAR STRUCTURES

Useful as they are, linear structures represent only a limited range of real-world relations between elements. A large number of these relations are more general and complex than can be represented by linear lists since they involve branching relationships rather than linear relationships.

PROCEDURE SORTLIST

```
procedure sortlist (var list : itemptr);
(* replaces unsorted list with sorted list *)

var   p, oldlist : itemptr;


  function successor (p : itemptr) : itemptr;
  (* returns pointer to successor of p *)

  begin
    successor := p^.link
  end; (* of successor function *)


  function predecessor (list : itemptr,
                        p : itemptr) : itemptr;
  (* returns pointer to predecessor of p in
     list. if p is first in list returns nil *)

  var   t : itemptr;

  begin
    if p = list   (* test if p is first in list *)
      then  t := nil   (* p has no predecessor *)
      else  begin
              t := list;
              while t^.link <> p do
                t := successor (t)
            end;

    predecessor := t
  end;  (* of predecessor function *)


  function largest (list : itemptr) : itemptr;
  (* returns pointer to point with largest x value
     in list.  note -- there must be at least one
     item in list!      *)

  var   p,t : itemptr;
```

```
begin
  p := list;  (* initialize temporary largest *)
  t := successor (p);
  while t <> nil do                  (* scan list *)
    begin
      if p^.x < t^.x        (* compare x coords *)
        then  p := t;       (* temporary largest *)

      t := successor (t)            (* advance *)
    end;

  largest := p                 (* value returned *)
end;  (* of largest function *)


procedure add (var list: itemptr;  p : itemptr);
(* adds p to list *)

begin
  p^.link := list;
  list := p
end;  (* of add procedure *)


procedure remove (var list : itemptr;
                      p : itemptr);
(* removes p from list *)

var   t : itemptr;

begin
  t := predecessor (list, p);
  if t = nil
    then  list := successor (p)
    else  t^.link := successor (p);
end;  (* of remove procedure *)


begin  (* procedure sortlist *)
  oldlist := list;
  list := nil;                (* initizalize list *)

  while oldlist <> nil do
    begin
      p := largest (oldlist);  (* find largest *)
      remove (oldlist, p);            (* remove it *)
      add (list, p)         (* add it to new list *)
    end
end;  (* of sortlist procedure *)
```

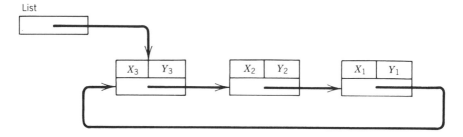

Figure 13.7. A circular linked list.

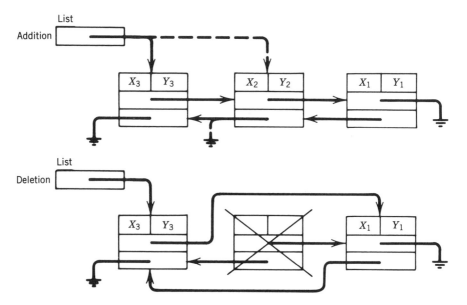

Figure 13.8. Addition and deletion of elements in a doubly linked list.

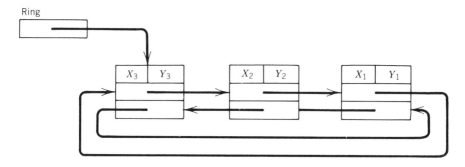

Figure 13.9. A ring structure.

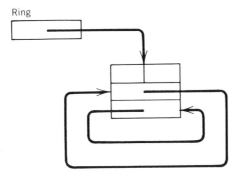

Figure 13.10. A ring with a single dummy element.

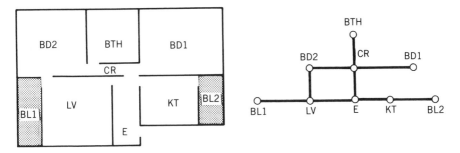

Figure 13.11. Graph representation of a floor plan.

Consider, for example, a representation of the traffic pattern or accessibility of rooms within a floor plan, as shown in Figure 13.11. This pattern is known as a *graph*.

Other useful nonlinear structures are *tree structures*, in which arcs may split but not merge, as is the case with graphs. Such structures, one of which is depicted in Figure 13.12, are useful for representing hierarchical relations. For example, a DRAWING can be considered to be made of a set of FIGURES, each of which is made of several LINES that, in turn, are made of a set of connected POINTS.

☐ SUMMARY

Linked lists utilize pointer types and record types to create a dynamic data structure; that is, a structure that can grow and shrink as needed during run time.

A linked list is accessed by means of a pointer variable called the *header* that

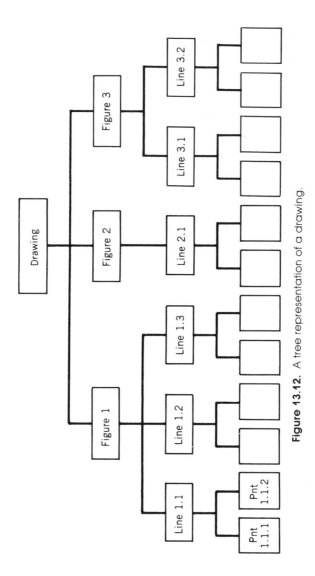

Figure 13.12. A tree representation of a drawing.

points to the first element in the list. Each element is a record, and one of its fields, a pointer variable called the *link*, points to the next element in the list. The link field of the last element in a simple list points to NIL.

One way to add a new element to a list is to make the link of the new element point to the first element in the list, and then swing the header to the new element, thus making it "first" in the list.

Traversal enables us to access the data in any element of the list. To traverse the list we create a temporary pointer, initialize its value to that of the header, and perform the desired operation on the first element. We advance the pointer to the next element and operate on it, and so on until we reach the end of the list.

One application of traversal is *hit testing*, which searches a list of graphic elements to find the one that the user indicated with the cursor.

To *delete* an element from the list we must swing the link pointers so as to bypass the element, then *dispose of* it. We must allow for the special condition at the head of the list.

A *sorting* algorithm arranges elements in order of some value. We can sort elements in a list by repeatedly traversing the list to find the largest value, removing that element and adding it to a new list.

Instead of using the simple NIL-ended list, it is sometimes helpful to use a *circular list* in which the last element points to the first element instead of NIL; or a *doubly linked list* in which each element is linked in both directions; or a *ring*, which is a doubly linked circular list.

Nonlinear structures involve *branching* relationships, in addition to linear ones, where one element may have a similar relation (e.g., be the predecessor) to *two or more* other elements. Typical nonlinear structures are *graphs* and *trees*.

14

EXERCISE 3

In this exercise you are to employ the various data structures that were discussed in this part of the book to store and modify drawings.

There are two distinct ways in which this can be done:

1. Use multiple different data structures, one for storing each of the figures the user can draw.
2. Use a single data structure, which is capable of storing all the figures.

As usual, no one of these two approaches is clearly superior to the other. The use of several different data structures is more prone to errors than the use of a single data structure, but dedicating each record to one type of figure may make the structure as a whole more efficient. On the other hand, a single data structure might be more general, allowing the future addition of more figures without necessitating major changes in the program. Yet, it may also waste much storage space because of the need to provide for parameters that are used in storing only one figure, but not the others.

Regardless of the approach you choose, it is recommended that you use one or more linked lists of records to store the data. This, of course, will support a variable number of figures drawn by the user, without imposing an upper limit (except for disk space), and without wasting unused storage space. It will also exercise your pointer-swinging skills that are so important for CAD.

Once stored, figures can be manipulated—erased or replaced. This is done by *removing* the stored figure from the list, and possibly by replacing it with another figure. To exercise this option, the user must be able to *pick* a figure, by placing the cursor on or close to the figure that is to be erased. A well-designed user interface will let the user know that the indicated figure has indeed been recognized by the system, by changing its appearance (e.g., its color or its line style—solid to dashed, etc.).

Using the hit-testing and picking techniques that were discussed in this part of the book, implement an "erase" utility for any figure that the user can place on the screen (the figures that were discussed in Exercise 2, Chapter 8). You may use the combination of CLEARSCREEN and REDRAW utilities to erase figures or an "undraw" utility to draw it in the background color (if your graphics drivers library supports this function).

PART FOUR

TEXT

15

ANNOTATIONS

So far we have concentrated on drawing lines on the screen and storing them in a data structure. Drawings, however, often contain text as well as lines. We call these items *annotations*. Their purpose is usually to clarify a figure or give it a name.

Annotations have two other important purposes: They can be used to identify the function of certain menu boxes, and they can be used to communicate messages and error conditions to the user at run time.

As we add functionality to the program and increase the number of menu boxes, it becomes difficult for the user to remember which operation is associated with each menu box. In Exercise 2 (Chapter 8) we used icons to illustrate the function of the menu boxes. However, not all functions are easily represented iconically. A simple label such as CIRCLE or QUIT would solve this problem.

Messages, also known as "prompts," are used when the action that the user is expected to perform is not apparent from the context. The judicious use of prompts may reduce the dependence upon lengthy user manuals and shorten the time it will take a new user to become familiar with the system.

In their capacity as error messages, annotations may let the user know why a certain operation has failed, so he will not repeat illegal or useless actions unnecessarily.

How can we produce annotations in a drawing or on the screen? There are two tasks involved:

1. We must specify the annotation as a whole—its size, its location, and the characters it contains.
2. We must draw, or otherwise produce, the individual characters that comprise the annotation.

For the second task we will rely on hardware-generated characters, invoked by calling an external procedure that produces the actual characters of the annotation. We could, instead, write a procedure for each letter of the alphabet, specifying MOVETO and DRAWTO to produce each stroke of the letter. But this would be quite tedious, and useful only if we wanted to generate nonstandard fonts (which we sometimes do).

There remains the first task. In this chapter we will see how to produce annotations and how to place them in the drawing.

☐ WHAT IS AN ANNOTATION?

An annotation is a string of characters (including blanks and punctuation marks) stored in an array. Because of the particular nature of characters, we can store them more compactly than numeric values by using the standard Pascal type called PACKED ARRAY:

```
type   textstring = packed array [1..30] of char;
```

In the above example we have a packed array that can hold 30 characters.

To assign an initial value to the text string that is stored in an annotation, we must use a two-step method:

1. Create the text.
2. Store it in an array.

One way to create the text is by declaring it as a constant:

```
const   msg = 'this is an annotation     ';
```

We can then store it by assigning it directly to a variable of type TEXT-STRING:

```
var   string : textstring;

begin
  string := msg
end;
```

Note that there must be exactly 30 characters in MSG, including blanks, to fill all the cells of array STRING.

Once the body of the annotation has been constructed and stored in a packed array of type TEXTSTRING, we can place it in the drawing by specifying its location, that is, the X,Y coordinates of the first character. We do this by means of an external procedure from our graphic drivers library:

```
procedure placetext (x,y,n : integer;
                     msg : textstring);
```

This procedure has four parameters: X and Y specify the location, a parameter N which tells how many characters in the annotation we want to print, and the annotation itself.

To place the annotation we created earlier at location 100,200 on the screen, we would use the following command:

```
placetext (100,200, 21, string);
```

The number 21 is the number of meaningful characters in this particular string. If we specify 2 instead of 21, only the first two characters will be printed, resulting in the annotation "Th". The value of N can be anywhere from 0 to the maximum number of characters in TEXTSTRING.

Procedure PLACETEXT allows us to use an easier method of creating the annotation. Instead of declaring it as a constant and assigning it to a variable, we can simply pass the literal annotation as parameter STRING:

```
placetext (100,200, 21, 'this is an annotation    ');
```

Let us now use annotations to place labels in the menu boxes we created earlier, so their purpose will be apparent to the user.

In Chapters 6 and 7 we used three boxes at the bottom at the screen for NEWLINE, CIRCLE, and QUIT. To label them, we will first create the body of the annotations as constants, then place each appropriately. Procedure LABELMENUBOXES performs these tasks. The result of this routine is shown in Figure 15.1.

PROCEDURE LABELMENUBOXES

```
procedure labelmenuboxes (output);
(* places labels in the menu boxes *)

const    msg1   = 'newline                    ';
         msg2   = 'circle                     ';
         msg3   = 'quit                       ';

var      string : textstring;

begin
   string := msg1;  placetext ( 50,20, 7, string);
   string := msg2;  placetext (400,20, 6, string);
   string := msg3;  placetext (750,20, 4, string)
end;  (* of labelmenuboxes procedure *)
```

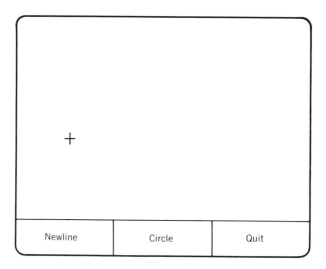

Figure 15.1. Using annotations to label menu boxes.

Generating Annotations Interactively

The annotations we placed so far have been constant annotations, whose body had to appear somewhere in the program. They are useful for labeling menu boxes and for conveying error messages to the user. However, the annotations that are most useful for CAD are those that are conceived by the user, rather than the programmer, and are used to explain parts of the drawing itself. Thus there must be a way to generate annotations interactively. We can still use Procedure PLACETEXT to place them on the screen, but both the location and the body of the annotation are now user controlled.

To create the body of an annotation the user must type it in, using the keyboard. We need some means to read the message and store it in our packed array. To perform this task we use yet another library routine called READ-TEXT:

```
procedure readtext (var n : integer;
                    var msg : textstring);
```

This procedure reads the characters typed by the user, until he terminates the string entry by hitting a carriage return (CR). The procedure then stores the string in the variable parameter MSG. It also counts how many characters were typed, storing that number in the variable parameter N.

Once the body of the annotation has been read, we must allow the user to determine the location of the annotation on the screen. This is accomplished by reading the cursor with a call to READCURSORLOCATION.

Procedure MAKEANNOTATION allows the user to enter a text string of up to 30 characters and place it anywhere on the screen by registering the cursor at the desired location.

As is evident in Procedure MAKEANNOTATION, a good interface lets the user know what he is supposed to do (when not obvious). It also regulates the screen location where the typed text is entered so as not to interfere with the drawing itself. In this example, the first call to PLACETEXT specifies a location at the upper left corner of the screen. READTEXT will automatically display the characters that the user types, beginning at the location where PLACETEXT left off.

PROCEDURE MAKEANNOTATION

```
procedure makeannotation;
(* prompts the user to enter a text string, then
   reads the text and places it at a user-
   indicated screen location *)

const   prompt1 = 'enter text:                   ';
        prompt2 = 'indicate location             ';

var     msg, string : textstring;
        n,x,y       : integer;

begin
  (* prompt user to enter body of annotation *)
  string := prompt1;
  placetext (10, 700, 12, string);

  (* read body of annotation *)
  readtext(35, 700, n, msg);

  (* prompt user to indicate location *)
  string := prompt2;
  placetext (10, 650, 18, string);

  (* read cursor and place annotation there *)
  readcursorlocation (x,y);
  placetext (x,y, n, msg)
end;  (* of makeannotation procedure *)
```

Storing Annotations

The annotations generated by the user become part of the drawing itself, and must therefore be stored along with the lines. We must set up the data structure in such a way that it will be capable of storing text.

The obvious choice for a data structure that can store the information that pertains to an annotation is a linked list of records. A linked list is warranted because we don't know how many annotations there will be, and a record is warranted because the information to be stored is made of different types—namely, text and integers. The following declaration is one possible structure to store annotations:

```
type    annptr      = ^annotation;
        annotation = record;
                        string : textstring;
                        length : integer;
                        x,y    : integer;
                        link   : annptr
                     end;
```

Procedure MAKEANNOTATION can now be augmented with code that will store the information entered by the user in an ANNOTATION record, and add it to a linked list of annotations (in the same way that we stored lines in a linked list). Thus, when the screen is refreshed and the stored information must be redisplayed, we can use the following Procedure SHOWANNOTATION to traverse the list and display all the annotations stored in it.

PROCEDURE SHOWANNOTATION

```
procedure showannotation (annlist : annptr);
(* traverses list of annotations and places them
   on the screen *)

var     ann : annptr;

begin
  ann := annlist;
  while ann <> nil do
    begin
      with ann^ do
        placetext (x,y, length, string);

      ann := ann^.link
    end
end; (* of showannotation procedure *)
```

Modifying Annotations

The user may want to modify the content or the location of annotations. To pick an existing annotation so that it can be edited or moved, we will use an operation similar to the hit test used for picking lines. This operation consists of registering a cursor location on the screen, then searching the list of annotations to see which one is closest to that location, within some predefined "range." The point

FUNCTION FINDANNOTATION

```
function findannotation (px,py : integer;
                         annlist : annptr) : annptr;
(* searches   the   list of annotations and returns
   pointer  to  the one closest to point  <px,py>.
   if all   annotations in annlist are out of range
   -- returns nil *)

const   range = 10;

var     ann              : annptr;
        dis, disclosest : real;

begin
  (* initialize returned value to nil *)
  findannotation := nil;

  (* initialize range of search *)
  disclosest := range;

  (* find closest annotation *)
  ann := annlist;
  while ann <> nil do
    begin
      (* compute distance of ann from <px,py> *)
      dis := sqrt(sqr(px - ann^.x) +
                  sqr(py - ann^.y));

      (* test proximity *)
      if dis < disclosest
        then begin
               findannotation := ann;
               disclosest := dis
             end;

      ann := ann^.link
    end
end; (* of findannotation procedure *)
```

that was used to place the annotation, that is, the X,Y coordinates stored in the annotation record, serves as reference. Function FINDANNOTATION performs this operation.

To relocate an annotation, we first call FINDANNOTATION, enabling the user to pick the annotation. Then we prompt the user to indicate another point on the screen and redisplay the annotation at that location using PLACETEXT. The new location must also be stored in the annotation record itself.

To change the body of an annotation, we again call FINDANNOTATION for the pick. The actual change to the text string can be implemented most simply by deleting the old one and entering another text string in its place.

□ SUMMARY

Annotations enable us to place text on a drawing or use text on the screen to communicate with the user.

An annotation is a string of characters, usually stored in a PACKED ARRAY. To place an annotation we call the external procedure PLACETEXT, specifying the location, length, and text of the annotation.

We can create the body of an annotation programmatically by declaring the text string as a constant and assigning it to a variable. Interactively, we can let the user type in a string of characters using the external procedure READTEXT.

Annotations can be stored most conveniently in a linked list of records. To *pick* an existing annotation for deletion or modification, we can search the list for the annotation that is within some predefined range of the screen location indicated by the user.

16

STORAGE

The lines and the annotations we have dealt with so far were stored in a data structure that allowed the information to be modified and redisplayed when the screen was refreshed. However, the nature of most design tasks is such that they cannot be completed during a single session. It may take weeks or even months to complete a design, and often several different professionals are involved in the process. How, then, can we store the emerging design over periods when the system is not running? The answer is to store the design in a kind of file known as a data file.

Data files are similar to the files in which we store the programs themselves. They differ from program files, however, in the way they are created and used. We do not enter data directly into them, as we do when we edit a program. Rather, it is the running program that creates and updates the data files by putting into them the lines and annotations created by the user. Data files are, then, intended primarily for the use of programs rather than human users. Still, it is sometimes desirable to inspect data files; therefore in this text we will make them readable by humans as well as machines. This will also facilitate their portability, though not necessarily the speed in which they can be written or read or the economy of the space required to store them. In this chapter we will see how to write and read text and store it in files.

□ WRITING

Pascal allows us to store data in files using the same statements that we use to write data onto the terminal in alphanumeric mode—the WRITE and WRITELN statements. WRITE and WRITELN differ from PLACETEXT that we encountered earlier in that they operate in *alphanumeric mode* rather than in *graphics mode*. They are not suitable, therefore, for use as means to display annotations, which are typically displayed when the terminal is in graphic mode.

They are, however, most suitable for use for writing onto *files* and in nongraphic programs that write onto the screen, or before the program goes into graphic mode and after it has left graphic mode (that is, before ENTERGRAPHICSMODE and after LEAVEGRAPHICSMODE).

The basic form of the WRITE statement is the word WRITE followed by a parenthesized list of arguments. The effect of the WRITE statement is to print the *values* associated with the arguments. For example, the statement

```
write(a,b,c)
```

will print the values currently associated with the variables A, B, and C. The type of each variable determines the type of the item printed. All four standard scalar types are printable, including BOOLEAN, for which the words TRUE and FALSE are printed. The values of expressions like (A + B) can also be printed.

In addition, we may print a string of characters that is not a value of a variable but rather a literal string enclosed within single quotes ('). For example, the statement

```
write('this is a message')
```

will print

```
this is a message
```

We can combine values and messages in one command. For example, Program SUM computes the sum of two numbers and prints the result. Note that the addition is performed *inside* the WRITE statement itself. The output of Program SUM is

```
the result is:        15
```

Note that an argument called OUTPUT has been added to the program name. It tells the compiler that this program communicates with some devices that are external to the program itself—in this case a device called OUTPUT, which stands for the terminal. In other words, this argument informs the computer that the output generated by the WRITE statements should be printed on the screen.

If we want to channel the output to a file or another output device, rather than the screen, we can do so using the following scheme:

1. List the name of the desired output file as an argument of the program. For example,

```
program sum (outfile);
```

PROGRAM SUM

```
program sum (output);
(* computes and writes to the screen the sum of
   two numbers *)

  const    a    = 7;
           b    = 8;

begin
  write ('the result is: ', a + b)
end.  (* of sum program *)
```

2. Declare the output file as a variable of type TEXT in the global declarations block of the program:

```
var    outfile : text;
```

TEXT is a standard type, whose full expression is

```
type   text : file of char;
```

3. Open file OUTFILE for writing, using the statement

```
rewrite(outfile)
```

The effect of this statement is analogous to rewinding a cassette tape and turning on the recording mode. It will overwrite anything that may currently be in the file.

4. Tell each WRITE statement to put the output in OUTFILE rather than the default OUTPUT:

```
write(outfile, 'the result is: ', a + b)
```

The output of the WRITE statements will now be sent to the designated file. Nothing will show on the screen; to review the content of OUTFILE, we have to print it out or enter OUTFILE with an editor.

WRITELN

Unless indicated otherwise, all the values given in WRITE statements will be printed on the same line, even if we use more than one WRITE statement. The following Program PRINT, for example, produces its results on one line.

PROGRAM PRINT

```
program print (outfile);
(* demonstrates the effect of formating on
   different data types *)

var     outfile : text;
        r       : real;
        i,j     : integer;
        c       : char;
        b       : boolean;

begin
  rewrite (outfile);

  i := 3;
  j := 2;
  r := i/j;
  c := '*';
  b := (i = j);

  write(outfile,'this is printed as: ', r,' ', c);
  write(outfile, (i div j), b)
end.  (* of print program *)
```

The output of Program PRINT, which will be stored in the file called OUT-FILE, is

```
this is printed as:_1.5000000e+000_*_____1false
```

(The underscores represent blanks.)

The output of Program PRINT is rather difficult to read, partly because everything is written on one line. We can improve the output by using the statement WRITELN to force a change to a new line at a suitable point. The rules of using WRITELN are identical to those for using WRITE. The results differ in that the output device moves to the beginning of the next line *after* printing the values associated with all the arguments in the WRITELN statement. If in Program PRINT we replaced the first WRITE with a WRITELN, the output would be

```
this is printed as:_1.5000000e+000_*
_____1false
```

Replacing the second WRITE with a WRITELN will not make any difference in the output since there are no more lines to be written by this program.

Formatting

If not specified otherwise, the *format*, or spacing, of the output will be determined by the computer according to preset defaults. The default format may be undesirable when we print integers or reals, especially when we want the output to be tabulated in a particular manner.

Pascal provides us with the means to control the horizontal spacing of each type of output (the vertical spacing is controlled by the WRITELN statement).

To control the output format of a value of type INTEGER we specify its *field width*. The field width is an integer or an expression that denotes the number of characters that the computer may use to print the value. In the statement

```
write(outfile, x:6)
```

where the value associated with X is 173, the formatted output will be

```
___173
```

If the field width is greater than the number of characters to be printed, the characters will be right justified in the field. If it is less than the number of characters to be printed, the field will be filled with asterisks (*) instead of the value.

Formatting is especially important when we print values of type REAL because the default format is scientific notation, such as 1.73E2, which is rather awkward to interpret. To control the format of reals we must specifiy both the field width and the *precision*. The statement

```
write(outfile, r:6:2)
```

for R = 1.73 will print

```
___1.73
```

The field width denotes the *total* number of characters, including the decimal point and the negative sign, if necessary, and the precision denotes the number of digits after the decimal point. Figure 16.1 shows the output produced by various formatting statements for a variable PI, which is associated with the value 3.1415926535.

The last statement in Figure 16.1 results in printing a single asterisk (*) in place of the value of PI, for it is impossible to print 10 decimal places, as specified for precision, in the specified field width of 1.

When we tabulate results and want to print suitable captions above columns of figures, it may be useful to draw out a typical line of output on graph paper. The exact spacing that is required may then be easily determined.

STATEMENT	OUTPUT

```
write(outfile, 'pi: ',pi);          pi:3.1415926535E+000
write(outfile, 'pi: ',pi:4:2);      pi:3.14
write(outfile, 'pi: ',pi:1:10);     pi:*
```

Figure 16.1. Formatting statements and their output.

Storing Line Information in a File

We can now utilize the WRITE and WRITELN statements to store the line information generated in an interactive session with the program. Typically, we will choose to store the data structure when the user is ready to terminate the session. To do so, all we need is to traverse the data structure and write out to a file the endpoint coordinates of each line or the parameters of an annotation.

Given a list of points that represent connected segments of a line, we can use Procedure STORELINES to write it out to a file called PROJECT.

The result of applying Procedure STORELINES to the group of lines shown in Figure 16.2 will be

300	200
200	300
300	100
100	200

PROCEDURE STORELINES

```
procedure storelines (list : itemptr);
(* writes endpoint coordinates of connected line
   segments in list to a file named project *)

var     l : itemptr;

begin
  rewrite (project);

  l := list;
  while l <> nil do
    begin
      writeln (project, l^.x:10, l^.y:10);
      l := l^.link
    end
end;  (* of storelines procedure *)
```

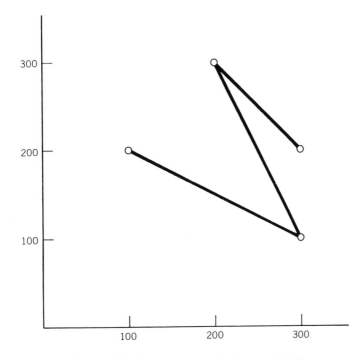

Figure 16.2. Storing connected line segments.

Program GRAPHICS in Chapter 18 shows how multiple disconnected lines can be distinguished in the output file by adding a code number to each pair of coordinate values. This code number identifies the first point of each line.

Naming Files Interactively

In most cases, users will have multiple drawings that they will wish to store in different files. In the former example, the name of the file had to be spelled out in the body of the program itself, thereby limiting the user to one output file of a predefined name (PROJECT, in this case). It is relatively simple to provide the user with the ability to *interactively name* the file in which he wishes to store the drawing, using the following scheme:

1. Let the user enter the name of the file.
2. Create a file with the user-defined name and open it for writing through the REWRITE statement.

The first of these two tasks is accomplished by Procedure GETFILENAME. TEXTSTRING is an array of CHARacters, like the one we used earlier for stor-

PROCEDURE GETFILENAME

```
procedure getfilename (var filename : textstring);
(* gets name of file from user input *)

const    maxchar = 30;        (* max filename size *)

var      i        : integer;

begin
  (* initialize file name with blanks *)
  for i := 1 to maxchar do
    filename [i] := ' ';

  (* get name of file *)
  write ('enter file name:');
  i := 0;
  while (not eoln (input)) and (i < maxchar) do
    begin
      i := i + 1;
      read (filename[i])
    end;

  readln (input)    (* consume carriage return *)
end;  (* of getfilename procedure *)
```

ing annotations. Here it is used for storing the name of the file entered by the user. It must, of course, be declared globally, such as

```
type   textstring = array [1..30] of char;
```

EOLN(INPUT) is a standard Pascal function that evaluates to TRUE at the end of an input line. It is used here to terminate the loop when the name typed by the user is less than 30 characters long.

The second task is accomplished by the following statement that associates the user-given name with the identifier used by the programmer in the program to denote the output file:

```
rewrite(project, filename)
```

Note the similarity of user-defined file names and programmer-selected file names to procedural arguments and parameters: The identifier PROJECT in the above statement is the parametric name of the file, as it is used throughout the program, while FILENAME is an array variable that is the argument (user-defined name) of the file that is to be associated with the parametric name.

Together, these two implementations provide the user with the ability to name the file into which the output of the program will be directed.

☐ READING

Reading data into the program in Pascal is very similar to writing it out, including the way the data is channeled to or from files. The READ statement, which is the counterpart of WRITE, takes the input (a number or a character) from the terminal and associates it with a variable that is given as a argument to the READ statement. For example,

```
read(a)
```

assigns a value that is taken from the terminal to the variable A. The variable A must, of course, have been declared earlier in the program and be of a type that matches the input value.

The effect of a READ statement is much like that of an assignment statement in that it assigns a value to a variable. The READ statement, however, obtains the values by interpreting data from the terminal or input file rather than by evaluating an expression that appears in the program itself.

When terminal input is used, the program will halt when it encounters a READ statement and wait for some value to be typed in by the user, followed by a carriage return. It will store this value and then continue execution.

We may read more than one value using a single READ statement by listing several variables within the parentheses. The statement

```
read(a, b, c, d)
```

will read four values and assign them, in order, to the variables A, B, C, and D.

The type of the values that are read must match the type of the variables to which they are assigned. If we declare

```
var   c,d : char;
       r   : real;
       i   : integer;
```

then the READ statement

```
read(c, d, r, i)
```

will expect two characters, a real and an integer, and assign them to C, D, R, and I, in that order.

We may read values of the types INTEGER, REAL, and CHAR only. BOOL-EANs may not be read, but it is easy to define the characters T as TRUE and F as FALSE, and interpret them as boolean values using a CASE or an IF statement in the program.

Format of the Input

When we enter integers and reals at the keyboard in response to a READ statement, we may put all or some of the numbers on one line, separated by at least one space or a comma. For example, the READ statements

```
var   r,s : real;
      i,j : integer;

begin
  read(r, i, j);
  read(s)
end;
```

will handle correctly any one of the following combinations of data:

  3.1 −16 15 −4.02E5

or

  3.1
  −16
  15
  −4.02E5

or

  3.1 −16
  15 −4.02E5

or

  3.1
  −16 15 −4.02E5

Note that the order of the values must match the order of the variables to which they are assigned.

When numerical values are read, spaces and new lines are ignored. When we read characters, however, each character represents itself—including blanks and line feed (new line) characters. Therefore, if we declare

```
var   a,b,c,d : char;
```

then the only way in which we can make sure that the values will be properly assigned is by typing in the input as

  PQRS

—no spaces, no line breaks.

Where characters are mixed with numerical values in a READ statement, spaces do count for CHAR type variables, but are ignored for INTEGERS and REALS. For example,

```
var   c,d : char;
      r   : real;
      i   : integer;

begin
  read(c, d, r, i)
end;
```

must be assigned data in one of the following formats:

```
      AB 3.1 −16
or
      AB 3.1
      −16
or
      AB
      3.1 −16
or
      AB
      3.1
      −16
```

Reading from a File

As with the WRITE statement, the default input for the READ statement is taken from the terminal. However, we can take input from a file instead, using the following scheme:

1. List the name of the desired input file as an argument to the program. For example,

   ```
   program data (infile);
   ```

2. Declare INFILE as a file variable in the global declarations block of the program:

   ```
   var   infile : text;
   ```

3. Open file INFILE for reading:

   ```
   reset(infile)
   ```

The effect of this statement is analogous to rewinding a cassette tape to the beginning of the tape. It will not affect the content of the file.

4. Tell each READ statement to take its input from INFILE rather than the default INPUT:

```
read(infile, a)
```

These provisions will result in taking the input for the READ statements from the designated file INFILE.

READLN

Since new lines and blanks count as characters when we are reading characters, what will be the value of D in the following Program READINPUT?

```
program readinput (infile);

   var   infile : text;
         a,b,c,d : char;

begin
   read (infile, a, b, c);
   read (infile, d)
end. (* of readinput program *)
```

If the format of the input values are

WXY
Z

then the answer is: ' ' (blank). The reason for this result is that breaking the input values by a carriage return is not sufficient to force the program to stop reading from the current line and begin a new one.

A similar problem occurs if we have some text on more than one line but wish to read only the first character of each line. Depending on the meaning of the first character, we may choose to ignore the rest of the line. We then need some means to interrupt the READ operation and go to the next line.

The solution provided by Pascal to both problems is the same: a directive in the program that tells the computer to ignore the rest of the input line and start reading values from the next one. This is done by the READLN statement. It is similar to the READ statement, except that *after* reading the input values for the variables within its parentheses, it will go the the next line. In Program READINPUT, if we change the first READ statement to READLN, the value of the variable D will be 'Z' rather than blank.

Retrieving Line Information from File

We can utilize the READ and READLN statements to retrieve the line (or annotation) information we stored earlier in data files. Typically, we will do so at the initiation of a session, thereby building up the data structure that existed in the previous session.

Given a list of points that represent connected segments of a line, we can use Procedure RETRIEVELINES to read them in from a project file named by the user.

The termination condition for the WHILE loop is the expression EOF(PROJECT). EOF is a standard function in Pascal. It evaluates to TRUE when we

PROCEDURE RETRIEVELINES

```
procedure retrievelines (var list : itemptr);
(* reads  the  endpoint  coordinate  values  of
   connected line segments from a file named by
   the user, and stores them in list *)

var     filename : textstring;
        l        : itemptr;

begin
  (* get name of project file  *)
  getfilename (filename);

  (* open it for reading *)
  reset (project, filename);

  (* initialize list header *)
  list := nil;

  (* read input and build list *)
  while not eof (project) do
    begin
      (* make new line segment *)
      new (l);

      (* read endpoint coordinates *)
      readln (project, l^.x, l^.y);

      (* connect new line to list  *)
      l^.link := list;
      list := l
    end
end; (* of retrievelines procedure *)
```

reach the end of the input file given as its argument. Without it we would not know when to terminate the loop, unless the number of iterations—that is, the number of lines—was known in advance. It is important to note that evaluation of EOF includes an implicit READ operation, to get the end-of-file marker. For this reason, if EOF is attempted when the file is empty to begin with, a run-time error will occur. Such error can be averted if the user directs the program *not* to retrieve information that does not yet exist or name the file he wishes to retrieve the information from.

☐ SUMMARY

To store a project between sessions of the program, we must write the project to a *data file*. A data file is written and read by the program itself, rather than by the user or the programmer.

The WRITE statement enables us to write out the value of a variable, or several variables, of type INTEGER, REAL, CHAR, or BOOLEAN. By default the values are written on the terminal screen. If we want the values to be written to a file instead, we must declare the file as a program argument and as a global variable of type TEXT, open the file for writing, and specify the file in each WRITE statement.

The WRITELN statement is like WRITE, except that the output device moves to the next line after writing the specified values.

To *format* the output of an integer we specify the *field width*. For a real, we specify *field width* and *precision;* otherwise the real will be written in scientific notation.

The READ statement is the counterpart of WRITE that performs input. It reads a value, or several values, and assigns each value to a variable. By default, input is taken from the terminal. We can read from a file by taking measures similar to writing to a file.

The READLN statement is the counterpart of WRITELN. After reading the specified number of values, it moves to the next line of input, ignoring any data that may remain on the current line.

The types of the values that are read by a READ or READLN statement must match the type of the variables to which they are assigned.

When reading integers or reals, the data must be separated by at least one blank or comma between values. When reading characters, every character represents itself, including blanks and new lines. Booleans cannot be read directly.

17

EXERCISE 4

In this exercise you will extend the scope of the utilities that are available to the user by including nongraphical (text) interactive annotations and by implementing the important features of storing and retrieving drawings.

These two utilities are closely related—they both make use of Pascal's read/write abilities. The major differences between them are the source and the destination of the data: Annotation are generated by the user and appear on the screen, while storage and retrieval of drawings is based on file manipulation.

To accommodate the first utility—user interactive text annotations—the data structure that you implemented in Exercise 3 (Chapter 14) must be extended so it can store text strings and their screen locations. Additionally, you should provide the operators to add and remove annotations, along with the appropriate user interfaces. It would help if you considered annotations as another kind of "figure," and approached them similarly to other figures.

To accommodate the second task—storage and retrieval of drawings—your program must be made capable of writing the data structure that has been generated during an interactive design session onto a text file, and capable of reading that file upon the initiation of a new design session, while rebuilding the data structure.

The user should have the option to discard the drawing—that is, not to store it in a file—and the option to direct the system not to retrieve a drawing at the beginning of a new session (such as when he wishes to start on a new project). Additionally, the user should have the option to *name* the file from which he wants to retrieve the project and the file in which he wants to store the current drawing.

18

CONCLUSION

In this text we have covered three important subjects:

1. The principles of problem solving with the aid of computers.
2. Programming in Pascal.
3. Simple interactive computer graphics.

We started with a simple problem: How do we draw a line on the screen of a graphic display terminal? Gradually, we progressed to more difficult problems—creating a menu-driven user interface, giving flexibility and control to the user, managing the complexity of the program, making the program readable and comprehensible to the programmer, and controlling the structure and storage of data.

In solving these problems we learned how to store and access data in memory cells, how to implement repetition and branching in the program, how to use abstraction and partitioning, how to define and use simple data types, structured data types, dynamic data structures, and text, and how to store data in files.

It is time now to consolidate all the components and see what we have accomplished. The principles and techniques that we learned allow us, in combination, to construct a simple yet functional drafting system. This drafting system does not provide all the functions that might be needed in a production drafting system, nor does it come close to Coons' scenario of an "intelligent" computer-aided design. Nevertheless, it does provide the capabilities of entering, modifying, and storing lines on a graphic display terminal.

Program GRAPHICS, which follows, embodies the knowledge we gained in this text. It provides the basic drafting capabilities for entering lines; it stores the lines in a data structure so that elements can be deleted; and it also writes them to a text data file for storage between sessions.

PROGRAM GRAPHICS

```
program graphics (input, output, project);

(* this is a simple graphics editor whose data
   base consists of lines, each of which is made
   of connected segments. it can create lines
   (made of straight line segments), delete the
   last segment entered and/or the last line
   entered, and redisplay the data base. upon
   system start-up it will retrieve the data
   stored in a file called project and rebuild
   the data base. upon exit it will store the
   data base in the same file, overwriting its
   old content.

   the menu consists of 18 boxes arranged in 3
   rows of 6 boxes each. only 5 boxes in the top
   row are currently used. each menu box is
   associated with a unique code, as follows:

   111     112     113     114     115     116
   121     122     123     124     125     126
   131     132     133     134     135     136

   procedure hittest returns this code, in a
   variable called box, along with the location
   of the cursor. if the cursor is not in any of
   the menu boxes, then box = 200. *)


const

   xfield        = 160;    (* pixels  *)
   yfield        =  30;    (* pixels  *)
   xmodule       =   6;    (* modules *)
   ymodule       =   3;    (* modules *)
   displacement  =   5;    (* pixels  *)


type

   lnptr        = ^line;
   sgptr        = ^segment;
   line         = record
                      lastsegment    : sgptr;
                      nextline       : lnptr
                  end;
```

```pascal
segment        = record
                   px,py         : integer;
                   nextsegment   : sgptr
                 end;


var

  database    : lnptr;
  menumap     : array [1..7, 1..27] of integer;
  project     : text;
  fileupdate  : char;


(*********************************************)
(*                                           *)
(*              menu operators               *)
(*                                           *)
(*********************************************)


procedure loadmenumap;
(* initializes menumap codes *)

var     i,j : integer;

begin
  for i := 1 to 7 do
    begin
      for j := 3 downto 1 do
        menumap [i,j] := 100 + 10*(4 - j) + i;

      for j := 4 to 27 do
        menumap [i,j] := 200
    end
end;   (* of loadmenumap procedure *)


procedure hittest (var x,y, box : integer);
(* returns menu map code and cursor location *)

var     i,j : integer;

begin
  readcursorlocation (x,y);

  i := ((x - displacement) div xfield) + 1;
  j := ((y - displacement) div yfield) + 1;

  box := menumap [i,j]
end;   (* of hittest procedure *)
```

```
procedure drawmenuboxes;

var     i,x,y : integer;

begin
  x := displacement + xmodule*xfield;
  for i := 0 to 3 do
    begin
      y := displacement + i*yfield;
      moveto (displacement,y);   drawto (x,y)
    end;

  y := displacement + ymodule*yfield;
  for i := 0 to 6 do
    begin
      x := displacement + i*xfield;
      moveto (x,displacement);   drawto (x,y)
    end
end;   (* of drawmenuboxes procedure *)


procedure labelmenuboxes;

const   box111 = 'newline                     ';
        box112 = 'del line                    ';
        box113 = 'del segm                    ';
        box114 = 'redraw                      ';
        box115 = 'exit                        ';

begin
  placetext ( 40,72,7,box111);
  placetext (190,72,8,box112);
  placetext (350,72,8,box113);
  placetext (520,72,7,box114);
  placetext (698,72,4,box115)
end;   (* of labelmenuboxes procedure *)


procedure displaymenu;

begin
  drawmenuboxes;
  labelmenuboxes
end;   (* of displaymenu procedure *)
```

```
(**********************************************)
(*                                            *)
(*              graphics  operators           *)
(*                                            *)
(**********************************************)


procedure drawpoint (x,y : integer);

begin
  moveto (x,y);   drawto (x,y)
end;   (* of drawpoint procedure *)


procedure drawcross (cx,cy : integer);

begin
  moveto (cx - 10, cy - 10);
  drawto (cx + 10, cy + 10);
  moveto (cx - 10, cy + 10);
  drawto (cx + 10, cy - 10)
end;   (* of drawcross procedure *)


procedure marksegment (s : sgptr);
(* draws  a   cross  at the center of segment s.
   note: there must be more than one segment in
   the line record! *)

var    x,y : integer;

begin
  x := round((s^.px + s^.nextsegment^.px)*0.5);
  y := round((s^.py + s^.nextsegment^.py)*0.5);

  drawcross (x,y)
end;   (* of marksegment procedure *)
```

```
(******************************************)
(*                                        *)
(*            database operators          *)
(*                                        *)
(******************************************)


procedure error (errornumber : integer);

const   out1 = 'database is empty          ';
        out2 = 'line is empty              ';

var     msg : textstring;

begin
  case errornumber of
    1 : msg := out1;
    2 : msg := out2
  end;

  placetext (25,780,20,msg)
end;   (* of error procedure *)


procedure initializedatabase;

begin
  database := nil
end;   (* of initializedatabase procedure *)


procedure newsegment(x,y : integer);
(* creates  a  new  segment  record in the data
   base, as part of the linked list of segments
   of the last line *)

var     s : sgptr;

begin
  new (s);
  s^.px := x;     s^.py := y;
  s^.nextsegment := database^.lastsegment;
  database^.lastsegment := s
end;   (* of newsegment procedure *)
```

```
procedure newline (x,y : integer);
 (* creates a new line  record in the database,
    and initializes its first segment to nil *)

var     l : lnptr;

begin
  new (l);
  l^.nextline := database;
  database := l;

  l^.lastsegment := nil;
  newsegment(x,y)
end;   (* of newline procedure *)


procedure makeline (var box : integer);
 (* creates  a  new  line,  which  is  made  of
    multiple segments. keeps adding segments as
    long as no other  menu  operator  has  been
    selected *)

var    x,y   : integer;
       first : boolean;

begin
  first := true;
  hittest (x,y, box);
  while box = 200 do
    begin
      if first
          then  begin
                  drawpoint (x,y);
                  newline (x,y);
                  first := false
                end
          else  begin
                  drawto (x,y);
                  newsegment (x,y)
                end;

      hittest (x,y, box)
    end
end;   (* of makeline procedure *)
```

```
procedure killsegment;
(* deletes last segment of last line record *)

var         l   : lnptr;
            s   : sgptr;

begin
  if database = nil
    then  error (1)
    else begin
           l := database;
           if l^.lastsegment = nil
             then  error (2)
             else  begin
                     s := l^.lastsegment;
                     l^.lastsegment :=
                               s^.nextsegment;
                     if l^.lastsegment  <>  nil
                       then  begin
                               marksegment (s);
                               dispose (s)
                             end
                   end
         end
end;    (* of killsegment procedure *)


procedure killline;
(* deletes last line from the data base *)

var      l : lnptr;

begin
  if database = nil
    then  error(1)
    else  begin
            l := database;
            while l^.lastsegment <> nil do
              killsegment;

            database := database^.nextline;
            dispose(l)
          end
end;    (*  procedure killline  *)
```

```
(********************************************)
(*                                          *)
(*              file operators              *)
(*                                          *)
(********************************************)


procedure getfilename (var filename :
                                    textstring);

const   maxchar  = 30;

var      i            : integer;

begin
  (* initialize filename with blanks *)
  for i := 1 to maxchar do
    filename [i] := ' ';

  write('enter file name: ');
  i := 0;
  while (not eoln(input)) and (i < maxchar) do
    begin
      i := i + 1;
      read (filename [i])
    end;

  readln              (* consume carriage return *)
end;   (* of getfilename procedure *)
```

```
procedure savedatabase;
(* writes  database  to  file.  each  pair  of
   coordiantes is written on one line, preceded
   by the codes 1 or 2.  1 identifies that pair
   of  coordiantes  as  the  beginning of a new
   line, and 2 as the end point of a segment *)

var      l          : lnptr;
         s          : sgptr;
         filename : textstring;

begin
  getfilename (filename);
  rewrite (project, filename);

  l := database;
  while l <> nil do
    begin
      s := l^.lastsegment;
      writeln (project,'1', s^.px,s^.py);
      s := s^.nextsegment;
      while s <> nil do
        begin
          writeln (project,'2', s^.px,s^.py);
          s := s^.nextsegment
        end;
      l := l^.nextline
    end
end;    (* of savedatabase procedure *)


procedure retrievedatabase;

var     k,x,y     : integer;
        filename : textstring;

begin
  getfilename (filename);
  reset (project, filename);

  while not eof (project) do
    begin
      readln (project, k,x,y);
      if k = 1
        then newline (x,y)
        else newsegment (x,y)
    end
end;    (* of retrievedatabase procedure *)
```

```
(*********************************************)
(*                                           *)
(*            display operators              *)
(*                                           *)
(*********************************************)


procedure displaydata;

var     l    : lnptr;
        s    : sgptr;
        dx,dy : integer;

begin
  if database = nil
    then  error (1)
    else  begin
            l := database;
            while l <> nil do
              begin
                s := l^.lastsegment;
                if s  <>  nil
                  then  begin
                          dx := s^.px;
                          dy := s^.py;
                          moveto (dx, dy);
                          s := s^.nextsegment;
                          while s <> nil do
                            begin
                              dx := s^.px;
                              dy := s^.py;
                              drawto (dx, dy);
                              s :=
                                  s^.nextsegment
                            end
                        end;
                l := l^.nextline
              end
          end
end;   (* of displaydata procedure *)


procedure redisplay;

begin
  clearscreen;
  displaymenu;
  displaydata
end;   (* of redisplay procedure *)
```

```
(*********************************************)
(*                                           *)
(*              user interface               *)
(*                                           *)
(*********************************************)


procedure getcommand;
(* user interface.  note:  'test' is used to
   eliminate extra hittest when user is done
   adding segments to a line *)

var     x,y,box : integer;
        test    : boolean;

begin
  test := true;
  repeat
    if test then hittest (x,y, box);
    test := true;
    if ((box >= 111) and (box <= 114))
      then case box of
              111 : begin
                      makeline (box);
                      test := false;
                    end;
              112 : killline;
              113 : killsegment;
              114 : redisplay
            end    (* end of case *)
  until box = 115
end;          (* of getcommand procedure *)
```

```
begin   (* main body of graphids program *)
  initializedatabase;
  loadmenumap;

  (* assume this is a new project *)
  fileupdate := 'n';

  write ('retrieve project from file? [y,n] ');
  readln (fileupdate);
  if fileupdate = 'y'
    then retrievedatabase;

  entergraphicsmode;
  displaymenu;
  displaydata;
  getcommand;
  leavegraphicsmode;

  (* assume database is to be stored *)
  fileupdate := 'y';

  write ('save this project? [y,n] ');
  readln (fileupdate);
  if fileupdate = 'y'
    then savedatabase
end.    (* of graphics program *)
```

☐ EPILOGUE

Two things should be kept in mind as we conclude this book, the first volume in a series of five:

1. This is a CAD book, not a Pascal textbook. Therefore, all the features of Pascal *have not* been discussed in it. Only those that were deemed most relevant to CAD, and in particular—to interactive computer graphics— have been included. Features that were left out include SET data type, VARIANT RECORD type, and GOTO control structures. The interested reader should consult a Pascal programming textbook about these features.

2. Interactive computer graphics alone, even when studied with CAD in mind, does not constitute computer-aided design. It only facilitates the *user interaction* with computer-aided design systems, which is of course a most important component of CAD. To make computers *design tools,*

they also need to be able to *represent* real-world artifacts and environments in a manner that is complete, well formed, and amenable to manipulation by the designer. Additionally, computers should be able to simulate the *design process* itself, such that they will become active *design assistants,* rather than mere passive repositories of data. Finally, to make computers *useful* design assistants, a host of *analysis, simulation,* and *tabulation* utilities must be added to the core representation and design process system, such that some of the design tasks can be delegated to or aided by the system.

These topics and others constitute the content of the four remaining volumes in this series, which together with this introduction span the principles of computer-aided design.

BIBLIOGRAPHY

The purpose of the following short bibliography is to provide interested readers with a lead to more extensive works in the four areas that have been discussed in this book:

1. The process of design, viewed from a computational stand point.
2. The programming language Pascal.
3. The design and analysis of data structures and algorithms.
4. Computer graphics.

The following books present principles, methods, and practices in their respective fields of specialization, and their lists of references can be followed to other relevant sources.

Simon, Herbert A.
  The Sciences of the Artificial (2nd ed.)
  Cambridge, MA.: The MIT Press, 1981.

Considers how a wide range of social, economic, political, and psychological systems can be coped with, adapted to, and understood by intelligent entities, such as human beings and "artificial intelligences." In particular, Chapter 5 is of significant interest to this series. It develops a logical model of the design process, using terminology and metaphors that were developed in or used by the field of artificial intelligence (search, reasoning, resource allocation, representation, etc.).

Jensen, Kathleen, and Niklaus E. Wirth
  Pascal User Manual and Report (2nd ed.)
  New York: Springer-Verlag, 1974.

A most authoritative reference book on the programming language Pascal, co-authored by the inventor of this language (Niklaus Wirth).

Wirth, Niklaus E.
Algorithms and Data Structures
Englewood Cliffs, N.J.: Prentice-Hall, 1986.

Focuses on the composition and analysis of computer programs, in terms of the structure of the algorithms and the representation of the data they use. The programming examples in that book are given in Pascal and in Modula 2.

Foley, James D., and Andries Van Dam
Fundamentals of Interactive Computer Graphics
Reading, M.A.: Addison-Wesley, 1982.

A compendium of principles, methods, and techniques used in the generation and representation of computer graphics images.

APPENDICES

A

KEYWORDS

The following keywords are reserved by Pascal for special purposes. The programmer may not use them as identifiers:

AND	DOWNTO	IF	OR	THEN
ARRAY	ELSE	IN	PACKED	TO
BEGIN	END	LABEL	PROCEDURE	TYPE
CASE	FILE	MOD	PROGRAM	UNTIL
CONST	FOR	NIL	RECORD	VAR
DIV	FUNCTION	NOT	REPEAT	WHILE
DO	GOTO	OF	SET	WITH

The following keywords are not reserved by Pascal, but they do have predefined meanings. The programmer should use them only in accord with those meanings:

ABS	EXP	ODD	READLN	SUCC
ARCTAN	FALSE	ORD	REAL	TEXT
BOOLEAN	GET	OUTPUT	RESET	TRUE
CHAR	INPUT	PACK	REWRITE	TRUNC
CHR	INTEGER	PAGE	ROUND	UNPACK
COS	LN	PRED	SIN	WRITE
EOF	MAXINT	PUT	SQR	WRITELN
EOLN	NEW	READ	SQRT	

B

DRIVERS

This appendix discusses the technology of graphic display terminals and the means by which programs can "drive" them.

☐ TECHNOLOGY

In general, a *cathode-ray tube* (CRT) works by heating up a metal cathode in a vacuum so that it emits electrons. These electrons are accelerated toward a phosphor-coated screen. The screen glows where the electrons hit it. By focusing the electron beam we can cause only one dot on the screen to glow, while the rest of it remains dark. By moving the focused beam, we can trace lines on the screen. The focusing and directing of the beam are done by electromagnetic fields, and the electrons are accelerated by means of applying high-voltage differences between the cathode and the interior of the tube, up to thousands of volts (Figure B.1).

The phosphor that coats the screen is usually of low persistence, so its glow decays quickly (usually 10 to 60 microseconds). In order to maintain a constant picture on the screen, it must be constantly refreshed; that is, the picture must be retraced at a rate of at least 30 times per second. If the refresh rate is slower, the picture will "flicker" noticeably.

There are two major techniques for refreshing the picture. One refreshes only the image itself and is called *vector refresh*, or calligraphic, display. The other one redraws the entire screen and is called *raster-scan* technology. Ordinary television sets are all raster-scan devices.

Each technology has its merits and drawbacks. Usually, a vector refresh screen allows higher accuracy of drawing. Raster displays allow color graphics and easy "painting" when an entire area is to be made to glow rather than a narrow line.

Points are plotted in response to digital signals from the computer. This

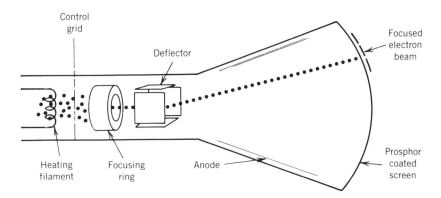

Figure B.1. The general composition of a cathode-ray tube.

means that they cannot be positioned with infinite precision; instead, we are limited by the precision of the values presented to the display processor. For example, if X and Y are passed to the display processor each as a 10-bit binary number (10 0's and 1's), there can only be 1024 (2 to the power of 10) distinct coordinate values for each. There are, therefore, 1024 × 1024 distinct positions on the screen where a dot can be displayed.

The resolution of the display is thus determined by the number of addressable dots per inch. For example, 100 dots per inch produces a better picture than 50 dots per inch. There are both upper and lower limits as to how many dots per inch can be displayed. If the eye cannot distinguish two dots that are less than 1/ 100 inch apart, there is nothing to gain by increasing the resolution to 200 dots per inch. On the other hand, it becomes rather expensive to build displays that are much larger than 12 inches square that contain 100 dots per inch, which means taking full advantage of a 10-bit address space.

Typical display processors have resolutions of 1024 × 1024 dots, but there are displays that can show up to 4096 × 4096 dots. By contrast, the typical home TV can show fewer than 256 × 256 dots.

☐ DRAWING LINES

Modern display terminals contain processors that are capable of computing the dots that should be illuminated, given the two endpoint screen coordinates of the line that is to be drawn. Therefore, we need only specify this pair of endpoints coordinates in our program.

Furthermore, display processors keep track of the *current access point* (CAP) at which the beam is located and require only the *destination point* (DP). In addition, they allow us to specify whether we want the beam moved to the DP while tracing a *bright vector* (a visible line) or a *dark vector* (an invisible line). In the case of color display terminals, we can actually specify the *color* in which the lines should be drawn, within certain limits.

The specification of the DP and the type of line drawn is captured by two primitive commands that we call MOVETO (X,Y) and DRAWTO (X,Y). The first moves the beam to the X,Y screen location without drawing a visible line, and the second draws a visible vector from the CAP to the X,Y screen location. Note that once the action is completed DP becomes CAP, so that subsequent commands start where the previous ones left off. By using these two primitive commands, we can draw any picture on the screen.

Throughout the book we used eight such procedures. We call them *display drivers* since they cause certain graphic display actions to happen.

☐ DRIVERS

Display drivers are usually unique to the hardware they were designed for; but some industry standards prevail. The small set of drivers we used in this text can be implemented in many ways. The following collection is one such particular implementation of these routines, as used by the author to facilitate the exercises in the book. They have been designed for the TEKTRONIX* family of terminals, and include, in addition to the eight main drivers, some global declarations and a utility routine that facilitate the implementation of the graphic display drivers.

*TEKTRONIX is a registered trademark of TEKTRONIX, Inc.

DRIVERS

```
(****************************************************)
(*                                                  *)
(*           GRAPHIC DISPLAY DRIVERS                *)
(*                                                  *)
(*        stored in a file named drivers.i          *)
(*                                                  *)
(****************************************************)


(* global declarations for the drivers *)

const

  maxchar     = 80;


type

  textstring  = packed array [1..maxchar] of char;


var

  cap          : array [(xlast,ylast)] of integer;



procedure writecoords (x,y : integer);
(* transmits a pair of coordinate values to the
   screen *)

begin
  write (chr(32 +  (y div 32)));
  write (chr(96 +  (y mod 32)));
  write (chr(32 +  (x div 32)));
  write (chr(64 +  (x mod 32)))
end;   (* of writecoords procedure *)


procedure clearscreen;
(* clears display screen while in graphics mode *)

begin
  write (chr(27), chr(12))
end;   (* of clearscreen procedure *)
```

```
procedure entergraphicsmode;
(* resets tektronix compatible terminal to default
   values, erases the screen then puts it graphics
   mode, thereby causing the commands sent by the
   host computer to be interpreted as graphic
   instructions rather than as text (same as
   clearscreen) *)

begin
  write (chr(27), chr(12))
end;   (* of entergraphicsmode procedure *)



procedure leavegraphicsmode;
(* returns terminal to alphanumeric mode *)

begin
  write (chr(24))
end;   (* of leavegraphicsmode procedure *)


procedure moveto (x,y : integer);
(* moves the current access position to location
   <x,y> by updating the global array cap to the
   new values   *)

begin
  cap [xlast] := x;
  cap [ylast] := y
end;   (* of moveto procedure *)




procedure drawto (x,y : integer);
(* displays a visible vector from the current
   access point (cap) to location <x,y>   *)

begin
  (* draw vector *)
  write (chr(29));
  writecoords (cap [xlast], cap [ylast]);
  writecoords (x,y);

  (* update current access point *)
  cap [xlast] := x;
  cap [ylast] := y
end;   (* of drawto procedure *)
```

```
procedure placetext (x,y, n : integer;
                       string : textstring);
(* displays  string  starting  at  <x,y>. n is the
   actual number of characters in string that will
   be displayed  *)

var     i : 1 .. maxchar;

begin
  (* moveto location <x,y> *)
  write (chr(29));
  writecoords (x,y);
  write (chr(31));

  (* write string *)
  for i := 1 to n do
    write (string[i])
end;   (* of placetext procedure *)




procedure readtext (x,y : integer;
                     var n : integer;
                     var string : textstring);
(* reads a text string from the  terminal,  and
   returns it and the number of characters read
   <x,y>  is the screen location where the text
   typed by the user will be echoed  *)

begin
  (* moveto location <x,y> *)
  write (chr(29));
  writecoords (x,y);
  write (chr(31));

  (* initialize string *)
  for n := 1 to maxchar do
    string [n] := ' ';

  (* read string *)
  n := 0;
  while (not eoln) and (n < maxchar) do
    begin
      n := n + 1;
      read (string [n])
    end;

  readln    (* consume carriage return *)
end;   (* of readtext procedure *)
```

```
procedure readcursorlocation (var x,y : integer);
(* reads and returns the location of the cursor on the
   screen *)

var      xhigh,xlow, yhigh,ylow : char;

begin
  write (chr(27), chr(26));
  read (xhigh,xlow, yhigh,ylow);
  readln;

  x :=  ((ord(xhigh) mod 32)*32) +
        (ord(xlow) mod 32);
  y :=  ((ord(yhigh) mod 32)*32) +
        (ord(ylow) mod 32)
end;   (* of readcursorlocation procedure *)

(* end of graphic display drivers *)
```

INDEX